PRICING DEPOSIT SERVICES

A Decision Making Handbook

L. Biff Motley

PRICING DEPOSIT SERVICES

A Decision Making Handbook

Bankers Publishing Company

Library of Congress Cataloging in Publication Data

Motley, L. Biff, 1946–
    Pricing deposit services.

    1. Bank deposits—Prices.   I. Title
HG1660.A3M645   1983   332.1'752'0681   83-11929
ISBN 0-87267-043-0

Printed in the United States of America

BANKERS PUBLISHING COMPANY
210 South Street
Boston, Massachusetts 02111

Executive Editor: Robert M. Roen
Production Editor: Nancy Long Coleman
Cover Design: Karen Mason

Contents

About the Author

Lawrence Biff Motley is currently a partner in the consulting firm of Whittle, Raddon, Motley and Hanks, Inc. which specializes in providing strategic management information regarding pricing, industry changes, new financial products and consumer marketing to depository financial institutions. He is responsible for the firm's research and product development effort as well as his direct consulting duties.

Mr. Motley holds an MBA degree from Miami University, Oxford, Ohio and has had extensive banking experience as an officer in commercial banking, marketing and product development at Continental Illinois National Bank. He has authored several other professional books in the area of new bank services.

Preface

If ever there was a time when it was necessary to know how to price and reprice deposit services effectively, now is that time. The 1980s have ushered in a new competitive spirit among depository financial institutions and other institutions competing for customer deposits. No longer can you sit back with the assurance that customers will come to you. You must attract them; and you must be certain that the services you use to attract them are profitable to your own financial institution.

How can you know how to price and reprice a service such as a money market account to make it both attractive to the customer and economically feasible for you? This text will give you the information you need. It is intended to be a working reference for the managers of financial institutions.

The first chapter discusses general pricing fundamentals, and the remaining chapters apply these fundamentals to a variety of deposit services. The purpose of each chapter is to present basic information that will help you obtain the information you need to make rational, profit-seeking decisions in an increasingly competitive environment. Each chapter covers a different deposit service and in each the focus is on costs, revenues, breakeven points, net income computation, and likely losses of accounts. Services covered are personal checking, NOW accounts, savings and CDs, and money market accounts. The last chapter covers the monitoring of other institution's services, pricing techniques, and policies.

The most popular feature of this text is it's easy to follow, step-by-step approach to help determine the need for repricing and the way to reprice. The detailed implementation guidelines for sample letters and sample forms and procedures are other useful features.

This book is designed to function as a tool to help you understand and price your institution's services more effectively. You must realize that for your institution to survive the turbulent 80s, you must price your services effectively and competitively. I hope this book will assist you to that end.

Introduction

This text relies on data developed by the Functional Cost Analysis program administered by the Federal Reserve Bank. The purpose of the Federal Reserve Bank's Functional Cost Analysis program is to enable participating banks to allocate various direct and indirect costs to the functions of the bank. Many times these functions closely approximate financial services.

The program is widely used and has proven to be an excellent tool in developing cost-oriented pricing strategies.

To reflect the impact of bank size on functional costs, the data in the Functional Cost Analysis is broken into three groups by deposit size: $0 – $50 million; $51 – 200 million; and over $200 million. Throughout most of this book, the functional costs used in the institutions were extracted from the $51 million to $200 million size group.

Interestingly, in many cases there appears to be positive correlation between bank size and functional cost levels, meaning the larger the bank, the higher the functional costs. It is my belief that this relationship exists because of the positive relationship between bank size, city size, and prevailing wage rates.

Much of the material in this book was developed from actual case studies. It is my belief that this information is accurate, projectable, and useful within the context of its presentation; and that the various pricing strategies thus developed are practical, workable, and sound. The figures used throughout this text are used as examples, however, and you should obtain the most current figures when developing pricing strategies for your own financial institution.

Every effort was made to set forth objective pricing approaches. If there has been any error in the development of pricing strategies and expected results, that error has favored the conservative end of the spectrum.

In spite of this desire to present simple, easy to understand pricing strategies and approaches based upon sound, objective data, there is a certain philosophical point of view built into the conclusions presented. This bias exists because of some of the concerns I have regarding the outlook for the financial services industry. Before beginning Chapter 1 it is a good idea to explore some of the factors that shaped my point of view.

It is my opinion that all growth must be profitable growth, lest the bank eventually strain its capital resources and weaken its ability to compete with an increasingly competitive array of suppliers of financial services.

We are living in a world of relatively diminishing capital, and financial institutions are facing competitive forces which will tend to place even heavier burdens on that limited capital. The financial institutions which demonstrate that they can generate sufficient future capital internally will stand the best chance of survival. It is my opinion that the best short- and long-run *marketing* strategy for a financial institution to follow is to optimize earnings.

The term "optimize" means taking a somewhat longer term perspective of a marketing and/or pricing strategy. For example, a financial manager might generate greater short-term profits by increasing prices substantially, cutting staff expenses, and spending no money on new product development or research. This approach might maximize short-term earnings, but might render the firm less competitive, and therefore less profitable, in the long run. Maximizing short-term earnings is an inappropriate strategy for an ongoing operation, while optimizing earnings insures not only short-term profitability, but continuity in that profitability. I use the term optimize advisedly, since to maximize short-term profits might foreclose the implementation of certain marketing programs that are necessary to attract profitable business. The key point is this: profitable current term operations insure that the bank will have the necessary economic power to survive in an increasingly costly and technologically sophisticated environment.

Given the basic financial and marketing objective of optimizing earnings, it is important to note two important conditions. First, financial intermediaries, such as commercial banks and thrift institutions, historically have been less profitable compared to other potential users of our country's increasingly scarce pool of capital. Moreover, looking at the financial industry as a whole, the average middle-sized bank (40 to 45 million) has a greater deposit growth rate (5.8%) than its growth rate of capital (4.1%). A generalized shortage of capital, if long lasting, could spell disaster for our industry. Second, there are forces at work which will increase operation costs even further. The elimination of Regulation Q; the introduction of various new deposit services designed to increase interest rates on consumer deposit; and the increasing costs of labor are all examples of trends which could further exacerbate earnings and capital adequacy problems.

The continuation of these trends will tend to eliminate the historic practice of paying less than market rates of interest on smaller accounts while "packaging in" the operational services performed on those accounts. In the future, financial institutions will pay interest on deposits closer to market rates, and will, *of necessity,* have to charge explicit fees for services performed on those accounts. Consumers learn more during each inflationary period, and in recent years the tremendous success of the money market investments has educated many people to *expect* money market rates on their deposits.

Given these trends, the pricing of deposit services assumes paramount significance to bankers. It is, indeed, one of the most important marketing considerations of the 1980s. The key question is how do we make sure that every customer is contributing to the bottom line? The answer is *through effective pricing.*

The title of this book is *Pricing Deposit Services* and a good financial executive will quickly ask, "What about loans? Can't they help offset the cost of low balance accounts?" This may be true, at least conceptually, but it is also inequitable. Market research performed by our consulting firm in over 90 communities nationally has demonstrated that while an excess of 90% of the families researched have *both* checking and savings, the percentage of families who have any sort of personal loan is far less. If a bank generally underprices its basic retail deposit accounts in an effort to attract potential loan customers, it could build in an operating loss among low balance accounts so that even attractive loan yields on the smaller outstandings associated with such customers would not render that segment of the account base profitable. Additionally, the phasing out of Regulation Q is likely to render a financial institution's cost of funds inhospitable to consumer-type loans, which by tradition are set at rate levels that assume artificially low costs and rate stability. The current national economic climate will result in sources of funds that are more costly than consumers expect and which contain so much rate volatility that dramatically new types of variable rate loans must be developed and sold to consumers.

All in all, the strategy of allowing borrowing customers to subsidize the costs of depositors is becoming more and more tenuous.

Moreover, in a world of capital shortage and higher costs, financial institutions should improve their overall loan and investment yields and deploy funds where they will provide the greatest net return. In the long run, banks should have comparatively little problem in finding profitable uses for funds. The challenge is to find profitable sources of funds. And it is to this subject that we now turn.

1

Checking Account Pricing — An Overview

The key to the effective pricing of personal checking accounts is to recover all of the activity costs associated with providing the service. Checking accounts are very costly to provide, and typically 70% to 90% of the number of accounts carry balances insufficient to recover costs. In this event a monthly service charge must be levied to recover the difference.

Market research studies reveal that 90% to 95% of all families have a savings account, money market fund, certificate of deposit, or other non-equity investment. The most popular types of "savings" today are the 6-month money market certificates, money market deposit accounts, money market funds, and regular savings accounts. And to a growing degree people tend to keep excess funds in these types of accounts which earn interest. Many of these people will keep this money at your institution, and the related balances (if large enough) can help offset checking costs.

So, before you increase your service charges, you should analyze the overall deposit profitability of your checking base. This procedure will be explored throughout the remainder of this chapter.

It is also probable that just as many (if not more) of your checking customers will keep their savings account at *another* financial institution. To recover their checking costs (assuming their balances are low), you must charge a fee. But you will also want to encourage these customers to bring you the accounts they keep elsewhere.

So, in summary, there are a number of purposes your checking service charge schedule should serve.

1. Recover activity costs
2. Distinguish between those customers who can and will pay in balances from those who must pay a fee
3. Encourage higher balances for both checking and savings

Some banks are located in very affluent communities where customers keep high checking and savings balances. Other banks are located in working class areas where people keep very low checking balances and are inclined to split their savings relationship. The bank in the affluent community can probably afford to underprice its checking account relative to activity costs since its customers will probably remain high balance customers. The bank in the working class area cannot. It must impose a service charge or it will be overcome by the operating costs of serving low balance accounts. But its service charge structure should also encourage its customers to bring additional checking and/or savings deposits to the bank. It is a more economical marketing strategy to convince existing customers to do more business with you than to convince noncustomers to switch.

PERSONAL CHECKING ACCOUNT COSTS

The following data was developed from cost studies of middle-sized banks ($50 to $200 million) nationwide, and it has been my experience that the "functional cost" of providing a checking account is fairly consistent among similar-sized banks.

The Functional Cost Analysis program (see Introduction for description) seeks to allocate the various costs associated with providing a particular service (e.g., a checking account) to the various functional components of that service. For example, a checking account is composed of several functions: processing home debits, processing deposits, clearing transit items, cashing checks, and maintaining the account on the computer with periodic customer account summary mailings. The total cost of providing these functions is then divided by the number of functions performed to give us the activity costs.

Activity	Activity Costs (rounded to nearest cent)
Process home debit	$ .12
Deposits	$ .24
Transit checks	$ .07
Account maintenance	$3.24 per month

Fixed and Variable Costs

To simplify our forthcoming analysis process, it is helpful to "load" all the transaction or variable costs (e.g., debits, deposits, transit checks) into a single "transaction cost." This transaction cost should be aligned in the customer's mind with "check writing," since this is the function most commonly priced.

Theoretically, one could charge for debits (check writing), deposits, transit checks, and account maintenance. But since common practice favors relating the variable costs to that over which consumers have the greatest control, it is helpful to "load" the costs of deposits and transit checks into the check writing cost.

Again, according to FCA figures, the typical personal checking account customers exhibit the following monthly activity:

Activity	Monthly Volume
Checks written (Home debits)	16
Deposits made	3
Transit checks deposited	9
Account maintenance	1

Combining the activity costs with the monthly volume for a typical customer would produce the following total monthly cost for a personal checking account:

Activity	Activity Cost	×	Monthly Volume	=	Total Monthly Cost
Check writing	$ .12	×	16	=	$1.92
Deposits	.24	×	3	=	.72
Transit items deposited	.07	×	9	=	.63
Account maintenance	3.24	×	1	=	3.24
Total Cost					$6.51

This $6.51 total monthly cost should now be divided into fixed and variable cost elements to produce a more equitable pricing mechanism. Even though the average customer writes 16 checks, some will write less and some will write more.

Additionally, there will be a positive correlation between check writing volume and the other variable costs associated with making deposits. The account maintenance cost will remain for every customer, hence it may be termed a "fixed cost."

To simplify our pricing mechanism, it is wise to combine the three variable costs (check writing, deposits, transit items), and to "load" them into the check writing cost.

To accomplish this we simply take the three variable costs, add them together, and divide by 16 (the average number of checks written).

Variable Activity	Variable Activity Cost	×	Monthly Volume	=	Total Variable Cost
Check writing	$ .12	×	16	=	$1.92
Deposits	.24	×	3	=	.72
Transit items	.07	×	9	=	.63

Total Variable Cost $3.27

Loaded Variable Cost = $3.27 ÷ 16 checks = $0.204
which would be $0.21 when
rounded up for a margin of safety.

In summary, we have now reduced our checking account costs to two categories:

Loaded cost per check written	$ .21
Fixed account maintenance cost	$3.24

This loaded variable cost then, is in essence the cost per check written which will recover all of the ancillary deposit costs when applied over an entire customer base.

Annual Cost

To obtain the average annual cost of a personal checking account, we simply multiply the monthly cost by twelve.

Activity	Activity Cost	×	Monthly Volume	=	Monthly Cost	× 12 =	Yearly Cost
Check writing	$ .21 (loaded)	×	16	=	$3.36	× 12 =	$40.32
Account maintenance	$3.24	×	1	=	$3.24	× 12 =	$38.88
Total					$6.60	× 12 =	$79.20

NOTE: The total monthly cost of $6.60 is slightly higher than the previous total cost of $6.51, due to rounding.

Historical Costs

Before proceeding to the issue of recovering costs, it is interesting to look at some historical cost figures related to personal checking accounts.

TABLE 1.   Cost Figures of Personal Checking Accounts

Year	Monthly Average # of Checks	Loaded Variable Cost*	Monthly Account Maintenance	Total Monthly Cost	Total Yearly Cost
1976	14	$1.82	$2.41	$4.23	$50.76
1977	14	2.24	2.46	4.70	56.40
1978	15	2.40	2.77	5.17	62.04
1979	15	2.85	2.98	5.83	69.96
1980	16	3.36	3.24	6.60	79.20

*Rounded

These figures imply an annual increase of about 12% in the cost of personal checking accounts. This is largely increased salary expense due to the labor-intensive nature of this function. Such dynamics argue for at least an annual review of checking account pricing.

SOURCES OF REVENUE AND BREAKEVEN ANALYSIS

A bank derives its revenue principally by investing depositors' funds (less any required reserves) in loans and other investments. In 1980, the typical middle-sized bank enjoyed the following yield characteristics on its earning assets.

TABLE 1.1   Average Net Yield on Earning Assets.

Use of Funds	% Gross Yield	% Operating & Acquisition Costs	% Net Yield Prior to Cost of Money	% of Earning Asset Portfolio	Weighted Average Yield Factor (Column 3×4)
Investments	10.56	.16	10.40	38	3.95
Real Estate	9.70	.75	8.95	22	1.97
Installment	13.15	2.89	10.26	15	1.54
Commercial	13.78	1.54	12.24	25	3.06

Average Net Yield on Earning Assets = 10.52%

This chart takes each major asset (or use of funds category) and defines its net yield, or value, to the bank. Let's review each asset category.

First, the investment portfolio. Based on Functional Cost Analysis data, the typical middle-sized bank was earning 10.56% gross yield on its investment portfolio. The operating costs associated with maintaining the portfolio (salaries, data processing, overhead) amounted to the equivalent of .16% (16 basis points) relative to the gross yield. So, after subtracting expenses the typical bank enjoyed a "net" yield of 10.40% from its investment portfolio. The table shows that 38% of the typical middle-sized bank's earning assets are in the investment portfolio.

Looking at the real estate loan portfolio, we see that the gross yield is the lowest of the four major categories. This 9.70% gross yield, while higher than in prior years, is improving more slowly than the other categories. The operating and acquisition costs amount to the equivalent of .75% (75 basis points), so the net yield is 8.95%. And the typical bank invests about 22% of its earning assets in mortgages.

Installment loans provide a gross yield of 13.15%; but with relatively higher operating costs (2.89%), the net yield is reduced to 10.26%. And about 15% of the typical bank's earning asset portfolio is invested in installment loans.

Commercial loans offered the highest gross yield (13.78%) in 1980 and with allocated operating costs representing the equivalent of only 1.54%, they also offered the highest net yield of 12.24%. About 25% of the typical bank's earning assets were allocated to commercial loans.

Taken together, these uses of funds produce an overall net *earning* asset yield of 10.52%. This weighted average is derived by multiplying the "net yield prior to cost of money" by the "percent of earning asset portfolio." In essence, this weighted average net yield is, to a bank, the value of its depositor's dollars.

This yield, however, must be reduced as it applies to the use of checking account funds since not every dollar provided by a checking account is actually invested in the bank's earning assets. Some of these dollars are in the process of collection; some are held as legal reserves; and some are allocated by the Functional Cost Analysis system to other non-earning assets, such as the bank's building. Taking all of these factors into consideration, the typical bank has about 74% of its personal checking dollars invested in earning assets.

Earnings Credit

The technical term used by bankers to define the value to the bank of its depositor's dollars is "earnings credit." This is the credit given to each customer for his or her deposited money. For personal checking accounts this figure is calculated by multiplying net yield on earning assets times the percentage of funds invested or $10.52\% \times 74\% = 7.78\%$.

Simply stated, every dollar that a customer keeps in his or her checking account and which can be invested for a year is worth 7.78 cents to the bank.

At issue now is recovering the annual operating costs of the checking account. This may be accomplished by maintaining large enough balances so that the earnings credit (in dollars) is at least equal to the operating costs. If insufficient balances are maintained, of course, fees need to be charged.

Breakeven Analysis

You may recover the $79.20 annual checking cost (see Table 1) by either investing balances or extracting fees. If you were to recover the entire amount via balances, a customer would have to keep an average balance of:

$$\frac{\$79.20}{.0778} = \$1,018$$

Or conversely, that customer could keep a very low balance (i.e., near zero) and pay you $79.20 per year or $6.60 per month. But while many people keep low balances, few actually keep a zero dollar average balance. So, we end up with a fee/balance trade-off. The higher one's average balance during a month, the less one should pay in fees.

This produces a variable fee schedule like the one below, where each $100 increment in average monthly balances reduces the required conditional fee by $.65.

TABLE 1.2   Variable Fee Schedule.

Average Monthly Balance	Monthly Earnings Value of Balance (7.78%)	Monthly Cost	Monthly Service Charge Required to Recover Deficit
$ 0	$ .00	$6.60	$6.60
100	.65	6.60	5.95
200	1.30	6.60	5.30
300	1.95	6.60	4.65
400	2.60	6.60	4.00
500	3.25	6.60	3.35
600	3.90	6.60	2.70
700	4.55	6.60	2.05
800	5.20	6.60	1.40
900	5.85	6.60	.75
1,000	6.50	6.60	.10

Looking at this table we can see that if, for example, a customer has an average monthly balance of $500, his or her earnings credit would be $3.25. Subtracting this amount from the average monthly cost it takes to maintain a checking account ($6.60), we arrive at the service charge needed to recover the deficit — in this case $3.35.

If one were to plot the fee/balance trade-off on a two dimensional chart, we can see clearly the multiple breakeven points defined by the particular combinations of fees and balances.

TABLE 1.3   Breakeven Fees Based on Average Monthly Balances

Monthly Fee										
7.00										
6.00										
5.00			Breakeven Balance/Fee Trade Off								
4.00										
3.00										
2.00										
1.00										
	100	200	300	400	500	600	700	800	900	1,000	Average Monthly Balance

So, if we are looking strictly at the checking account, a customer breaks even when he or she pays $6.60 per month. And this payment may occur through the maintenance of $1,018 in average balances or through an explicit fee of $6.60 or some middle ground combination of the two.

Savings Balances

Many customers choose to keep their checking balances very low and put excess dollars into a savings account. And this savings account can also be invested in the earning asset portfolio. The earnings potential of this balance is reduced, however, due to the fact that interest must be paid to the customer.

In theory, a financial institution should be indifferent as to whether customers elect to keep their "compensating balance" in a checking account, a savings account, or a certificate of deposit. As long as the earnings credit from the customers' balances are high enough to cover the costs of the account plus a profit, customers should be free to keep their deposits in any type of account.

If, however, customers choose to keep their money in a regular savings account paying, say, 5½% interest, then obviously the balances must be higher than if the money were held in a checking account paying no interest. Again, FCA data is helpful in determining this alternative balance requirement.

In 1980, the typical regular savings account had annual operating costs of $30.22. Given our 10.52% average net yield on earning assets and the FCA finding that about 95% of a bank's savings deposits are invested in earning assets (net of float, reserves, and allocation to non-earning assets), we end up with an "earnings credit" of 9.99%.

If we then subtract our interest cost of 5½% from this 9.99%, we end up with a spread (or interest margin) of 4.49%. This is the true value to the bank of its regular savers' deposits.

If we now divide this net interest margin into the annual operating costs associated with a regular savings account, we have the breakeven balance required to cover savings account operating costs.

$$\frac{\text{Annual Operating Costs}}{\text{Net Interest Margin}} = \begin{array}{l}\text{Breakeven balance to}\\ \text{cover savings account}\\ \text{operating costs}\end{array}$$

Example:

$$\frac{\$30.22}{9.99\% - 5.50\%} = \$673.05$$

So, the typical savings customer must keep $673.05 in his or her account (average balance) before the operating costs are paid for.

Let's say, though, that a customer keeps well in excess of $673 in a savings account. The earnings credit on excess balances would help pay for the operating costs of a checking account (or any other service for that matter). Of course they would, but how much should a customer keep? We can use the same breakeven analysis to make this determination. Let's simply divide the annual checking account operating costs by the net interest margin associated with the customers' savings balances.

$$\frac{\$79.20}{9.99\% - 5.50\%} = \$1,725$$

This $1,725 is required in savings, then, to pay for checking account activity costs. We must keep in mind that it takes $673 in savings to pay for savings account activity costs. So, when we add the two, we get $2,398, the total amount a customer must keep in savings to pay for both checking and savings.

In practice, the figure is often rounded to $2,000 or $2,500 to make the offer more simple; something like "You may have a free checking account for $2,000 in savings." The decision to round the figure above or below the true breakeven cost is made on the basis of the bank's overall growth vs. earning objectives.

Relationship Pricing

This idea of allowing customers to defray the costs of one service with the earnings on another is an example of relationship pricing. In theory, any combination of services may be combined from both a cost and a revenue point of view, and so long as all costs are fully covered, you have a profitable relationship.

Some feel that such an approach might actually reduce profits and a bank would be better off if all individual products were priced to render a profit separately. Advocates of relationship pricing argue, on the other hand, that unless pricing takes into account a customer's whole relationship, the bank is vulnerable to pricing competition, which may become even more severe during deregulation as financial institutions become more similar. These people argue that free markets tend to squeeze out any excess profit, and that over the long run a bank's smartest strategy would be to develop pricing mechanisms that encourage and protect a customer's total relationship.

Now, not all customers have a $2,398 savings account. In fact, studies performed by the consulting firm of Whittle, Raddon, Motley & Hanks, Inc., suggest that although 90% of your checking customers may have a savings account, only 50% are likely to have one with you; and those who do are likely to have an average balance of around $1,600. Moreover, your low balance checking customers are likely to have low balance savings accounts.

Nevertheless, you want your customers' savings deposits, and you may feel obligated to offer some fee reduction incentive to get them. One way to do this is to simply offer free checking to anyone who keeps, say, $2,500 in savings. Some of the West Coast banks have come up with such "saver's club" plans and are doing quite well in the highly urban markets.

In smaller markets you may want to consider some plan to give some credit for lesser savings deposits. Since each $1,000 in savings (after the first $673 which pays for savings activity) is worth 4.49% to your bank (or $3.75 per month), you may want to reduce a checking customer's monthly fee for each $500 to $1,000 he or she keeps beyond the $1,000 minimum. A simple plan would be to reduce a customer's monthly checking fee by $3.00 for each $1,000 (beyond the first $1,000) minimum balance maintained in a regular (5½%) savings account. And since the total monthly cost of a checking account is roughly $6.00 ($6.60 to be exact), then the customer would have to keep $3,000 in savings. The first $1,000 pays for savings operating costs; the next $2,000 pays for checking operating costs.

As you can see, this approach of giving a customer $3.00 credit toward service charges for each $1,000 in savings, above the initial $1,000, is a little simpler from a customer's viewpoint than the early breakeven approach. And since some of the figures were rounded, the resulting balances are a little higher.

An approach that is even more simple is to offer customers no service charge checking for a single round figure of $2,000, $2,500, or $3,000 in savings. This approach is the simplest of all, but sacrifices the ability to exact charges on those higher activity customers whose monthly fees might exceed the $6.00 on which such a plan is promised.

Breakeven Price — Core Deposit Services

This analysis leads us to a breakeven price structure for core deposit services. The term core deposit services here means checking and savings. Over 90% of your customers have these services, and since the industry currently pays "sub-market" rates for these deposits, they are also worth something as an offset against activity costs.

Given these facts, the following might be an appropriate breakeven price structure for a bank whose customers exhibit normal activity and who only have a checking account.

Minimum Monthly Checking Balance	Monthly Fee
$0–$100	$5.00
$101–$200	$4.00
$201–$300	$3.00
$301–$400	$2.00
$400+	No Charge

From a marketing point of view, it is highly desirable to price a checking account on the basis of *minimum* rather than *average* balance. It is simpler to understand and has the distinct advantage of appearing lower than comparable average balances.

This schedule is based upon the relationship between average balance and minimum balance as shown in Table 1.4.

TABLE 1.4   Relationship Between Average and
Minimum Balance

Average Balance Range $	Average Balance $	Minimum Balance $	Average ÷ Minimum $
1–100	44	10	3.9
101–200	149	40	3.9
201–300	250	90	2.8
301–400	350	160	2.2
401–500	451	225	2.0
501–600	550	275	2.0
601–1,000	740	420	1.7
1,001–1,500	1,212	790	1.5
1,501–2,500	2,000	1,428	1.4

Source: Surveys conducted by consulting firm of Whittle, Raddon,
Motley & Hanks, Inc.

As can be seen from this table, people who keep less in their
checking account exhibit greater volatility in the relationship between average and minimum balance levels. This is logical when one
thinks about it since people who maintain a low balance would tend to
exhaust a higher proportion of their total account with everyday
checkwriting than someone who kept a large balance.

For example, take someone whose minimum balance might
have dropped to $100 during the month. Such a person might have
made two or three deposits of maybe $400 to $500 and written 15
checks. Since their lowest balance was $100, their average daily
balance was obviously higher. In my experience, this relationship
between a checking account's minimum balance and its average
balance is curvilinear and ranges from a ratio of 3.9 to 1 for lower
balance accounts, to 1.4 to 1 for higher balance accounts.

If someone's minimum balance had fallen below $100, then their average balance would be in the $200 to $300 range. Since, as we determined earlier, the annual earnings credit on a checking account is 7.78% (10.52% net yield less float and reserves), the monthly earnings credit would be 7.78% ÷ 12, or .648%. This monthly factor applied to $200 is $1.30, and applied to $300 is $1.94. So, this customer's balance is worth between $1.30 and $1.94 to the bank. For simplicity, let's say the average balance is $250 and the earnings credit is $1.60.

As we remember, the monthly operating costs associated with this account total $6.60. This leaves $5.00 in costs uncovered by balanced related revenues, hence a monthly service charge of $5.00 is appropriate.

Since some people elect to maintain higher balances, then their fees should be correspondingly less. For each $100 of average balance, the bank obtains $.648 in revenue to defray operating costs. And it takes 10.2 of these $100 increments (or about $1,000 average balance) to totally defray the $6.60. As we can see, then, from the Average vs. Minimum Balance Chart (Table 1.4), this $1,000 average balance corresponds to a $417 minimum balance. So, the bank can offer no service charge checking provided the minimum does not fall below that level.

In practice, this no charge minimum is often rounded to either $400 or $500 depending on the bank's earnings and/or growth objectives relative to its market.

Why Minimum Balances

Many bankers wonder if it is worth the trouble to convert average balances to minimums. Why not simply price on the basis of a customer's average balance?

There are two basic reasons. First, people do not relate to their average balance, but easily understand the concept of minimum balance or low monthly balance. Second, most people cannot distinguish between a balance requirement expressed in averages versus one expressed in minimums. So the minimums always appear lower.

Consumer research done by the firm of Whittle, Raddon, Motley & Hanks, Inc. consistently confirms that consumers prefer minimum balance plans. In fact, banks competing with many of our clients have attempted to attract new business by offering a lower and more fair pricing structure of, say, no charge for $500 average balance, while our client maintained a $400 minimum. And to the competitor's chagrin, not only did the strategy fail, but they actually lost customers who felt that the $500 average was a $500 minimum.

The point is that consumers think in terms of low balances anyway. So a bank's pricing structure should reflect this preference.

Silent Parameter To Protect Higher Balance Customers

Pricing on minimums can be unfair to that handful of higher balance customers who maintain very profitable average balances but whose minimums might fall below the threshold level. Frequently, to solve this problem, banks program their computers to waive the monthly service charge if, for example, either the minimum exceeds $500 or the average exceeds $1,000.

The higher average balance parameter is often not even published, but put in as a sort of "fail safe" to protect the higher balance customer.

Single Minimum vs. Variable Minimum

Given the figures we've been looking at, some banks will use a variable minimum balance pricing structure.

Minimum Monthly Balance	Monthly Fee
$0–$100	$5.00
$101–$200	$4.00
$201–$300	$3.00
$301–$400	$2.00
+$400	No Charge

Others will use the simpler single minimum balance.

Minimum Monthly Balance	Monthly Fee
$0–$400	$5.00
+$400	No Charge

The decision to use one or the other is a strategic (i.e., competitive) one. And while it will be explored more fully later in this chapter, it might be helpful to look at some of the relative advantages of each plan.

TABLE 1.5   Advantages of Single and of Variable Minimum Balance Plans

Single	Variable
• Easier to understand if your pricing is lower.	• Less directly comparable if your pricing is higher.
• Emphasizes specific threshold balance requirement.	• Emphasizes the general idea that the more a customer keeps, the less he or she pays.
• Simpler.	• More equitable.

More will be said about this and other pricing structures later, but for now we should turn to the issue of *your* particular account base. The data presented thus far is average data reflecting the practices of many banks who participate in the Fed's Functional Cost Analysis Program. And while given the state of the art in bank data processing and operations there may be very little variation in checking costs, there are some significant variations.

1. *Average Activity*
   This has ranged from as few as 10 checks per month to as many as 50, depending upon the area of the country and the type of checking plan.
2. *Balance Range Stratification*
   The proportion of total accounts and balances under various average and minimum balances.
3. *Savings Cross-sell*
   The percentage of checking customers who have savings has ranged from as few as 30% to as high as 70%.

These factors can have a significant effect on your bank's pricing strategy and structure. If, for example, your customers exhibit high balances and low activity, you may engage a relatively low service charge strategy. While if customer balances are low, activity high, and if your capacity is strained, you may choose to charge well above breakeven to recover costs and to export unprofitable business elsewhere.

ACCOUNT BASE PROFITABILITY

To determine your bank's best pricing structure, you'll have to sample your account base. You are looking for the following key information:

- percent of customers in various average balance categories
- average monthly activity
- average monthly fee income
- percent of customers with savings and average balances
- percent of customers with other services (mortgages, CDs, installments, etc.) This data may not be used to set checking fees, but is an important index of overall cross-sell effectiveness.

Sampling Format

Your sample should be structured to provide you with data arranged into the format shown in Table 1.6.

TABLE 1.6   Format to Determine Account Base Profitability

Average Monthly Checking Balance	# in Sample	% of Total Sample	Median # of Transactions (Checks)	Average Monthly Fee Income	% With Savings	Median Savings Balance
0–100						
101–200						
201–300						
301–400						
401–500						
601–999						
1,000+						

This format is based upon the primary retail services. You may, however, want to include other services such as mortgages or bank charge card that have meaningful profit implications for your personal checking customer base. The purpose of such a grid is to determine the degree of cross-selling required to recapture losses from unprofitable checking accounts (if any). It is most important that this type of data be developed for *different average balance amounts* since the average balance a person maintains in a checking account often reflects the use of other bank services.

Sampling Procedure

To build this matrix you should randomly sample your checking account base. If your bank offers more than one checking plan, you should sample all of them, making sure to keep the samples separate. This will allow comparisons to be made.

Since there is such a wide variation in activity, you should sample your demand deposit accounts (DDA) customer base to obtain your average activity (i.e., checks written per month).

This sample should be between 1% and 5% of your account base (but at least 300), and you must pick each account at random. To ensure that you get a true random sample, take every "Nth" account from your master file, where

$$N = \frac{\text{Account Base}}{\text{Sample Size}}$$

For example, if you have 10,000 personal checking accounts and you want a sample of 500 (5%), you should choose every 20th name. This is called your sample interval.

Sampling Work Sheet

For every name, then, in the sample, you should fill out a work sheet similar to the example shown in Exhibit 1. It should be constructed to include the services that are most important to you. After you have completed the sample, the sheets should be *organized by checking balance category* so the appropriate averages may be obtained.

EXHIBIT 1   Sampling Work Sheet

Account # _____

Account Name _____

1. Checking Account Average Balance (Circle One)

0–100	301–400	601–700	901–1,000
101–200	401–500	701–800	over 1,000
201–300	501–600	801–900	

2. Average Monthly Transactions _____

3. Monthly Fee Income _____

EXHIBIT 1. *(continued)*

---

4. Regular Savings Account (One or More)

   1 — Yes   2 — No

5. Balance in Savings Account (if name has more than one savings
   account, include Total Balance) (Circle One)

0–100	401–500	801–900	2,001–5,000
101–200	501–600	901–1,000	5,001–10,000
201–300	601–700	1,001–2,000	over 10,000
301–400	701–800		

6. 90 Day Savings

   1 — Yes   2 — No

7. 90 Day Balance _____

8. C/D

   1 — Yes   2 — No

9. C/D Balance _____

10. Installment Loan

   1 — Yes   2 — No

11. Bank Charge Card

   1 — Yes   2 — No

12. Mortgage Loan

   1 — Yes   2 — No

A Note on the Use of Averages

In banking, it is important that averages be as reflective of the greatest
number of customers as possible. For this reason, wherever possible,
we will use *median* averages rather than *mean* averages since they are

a more reliable measure and less subject to the distortions of unusually large or small accounts.

Customer Profile

The Customer Profile is produced from your sample to give you a bird's eye view of your checking account customer base. This chart is developed by sorting your sample into relevant average balance size groups such as:

0–100, 101–200, 201–300, 301–400, 401–500, 501–600, 601–999, 1,000+

You can use as many as you wish, but as you get toward the upper end (higher balances) you might begin broadening the ranges. In our example, when we reached the $600 average balance range, we extended it to $999. This is done to simplify your job, since checking pricing tends to focus more definitely on the low balance end of the spectrum.

TABLE 1.7 Sample Customer Profile

Average Balance Range	# of Accounts	% of Accounts	Median # Trans. (Checks)	Median Service Charge	% With Savings	Median Savings Balance	Other Services
0–100	130	26	15	3.42	22	50	
101–200	135	27	18	2.88	26	250	
201–300	25	15	19	1.99	35	300	
301–400	20	4	19	.85	39	400	Include
401–500	15	3	17	.25	42	650	As
501–600	25	5	15	.10	55	950	Desired
601–999	40	8	14	.00	61	1,800	
1,000+	60	12	13	.00	65	2,200	
TOTAL	500	100	16	2.50	38	1,000	

Profitability Analysis

This important sample data is then combined with the previously developed cost data to form the chart (annual data) shown in Table 1.8.

TABLE 1.8   Net Profit Per Account Per Year ($)

							Core
			Checking			Savings	Deposits
						Net	Earnings
Average	Portfolio	+ Service	− Cost	= Profit		Savings	Checking
Balance	Income	Fees				Earnings	& Savings
0–100	3.89	+ 41.04	− 76.68	= (31.75)		.00	(31.75)
101–200	11.67	+ 34.56	− 84.24	= (38.01)		.00	(38.01)
201–300	19.45	+ 23.88	− 86.76	= (43.43)		.00	(43.43)
301–400	27.23	+ 10.20	− 86.76	= (49.33)		.00	(49.33)
401–500	35.01	+ 3.00	− 81.72	= (43.71)		.00	(43.71)
501–600	42.79	+ 1.20	− 76.78	= (35.69)		12.44	(23.25)
601–999	58.35	+ .00	− 74.16	= (15.81)		50.60	34.79
1,000+	116.70	+ .00	− 71.64	= 45.06		68.56	113.62

Data offered for illustrative purposes

Definitions:

1. *Portfolio Income*
    Use 7.78% or your own net earnings credit × the middle of the average balance range (i.e., $50, $150, $250 — for the $1,000+ category use $1,500).
2. *Service Fee*
    Use your own data developed from your sample. Be sure to annualize the data.
3. *Cost*
    Use FCA data for your bank size, or our example data of $.21 per check plus $38.88 account maintenance.
4. *Net Savings Earnings*
    Exempt the first $673 of each category's median balance (e.g., if it's $3,000, subtract $625). This, as you

recall, is the balance required to pay for savings account activity costs. Multiply resultant figure by 4.49%, or your interest margin on savings accounts. (Since the purpose of this analysis is to recover checking costs, we do not consider actual losses on savings accounts. The pricing of savings accounts and their value as an offset to checking fees will be treated later.)

5. *Annual Earnings Checking and Savings*
    Add checking and savings earnings.

Analysis of "Net Profit Per Account Per Year"

Table 1-8 clearly indicates that annual checking account costs exceed both fee and balance related revenues for all balance categories except the over $1,000 group. In fact, the middle ranges lose even more money because of their higher activity costs and lower service charges.

If we were to take the checking profit column, shown in Table 1.9, and divide by 12, we would have an approximation of both the monthly loss and the necessary increase in service charges required to break even.

TABLE 1.9   Service Charge Required to Break Even on Checking Costs

Average Balance ($)	Annual Checking Profit (Loss) ($)	÷ 12 =	Monthly Profit (Loss) ($)
0–100	(31.75)		(2.65)
101–200	(38.01)		(3.17)
201–300	(43.43)		(3.62)
301–400	(49.33)		(4.11)
401–500	(43.71)		(3.64)
501–600	(35.69)		(2.97)
601–999	(15.81)		(1.32)
1,000+	45.06		3.76

A similar analysis might be done on the last column, "earnings checking and savings."

TABLE 1.10   Service Charge Required to Break Even on Checking/Savings Accounts

Average Balance ($)	Annual Earnings (Loss) Checking/Savings ($)	÷ 12 =	Monthly Earnings (Loss) Checking/Savings ($)	
0–100	(31.75)		(2.65)	
101–200	(38.01)		(3.17)	Same
201–300	(43.43)		(3.62)	as
301–400	(49.33)		(4.11)	Above
401–500	(43.71)		(3.64)	
501–600	(23.25)		(1.94)	
601–999	34.79		2.87	
1,000+	113.62		9.47	

As we can see, based on the addition of net savings earnings, only those accounts with over $500 average balances were improved. And, in general, all deposit size groups below $600 are unprofitable and in need of higher service charges. Referring to our "minimum vs. average balance" chart (Table 1.4), we can see that a $600 average balance relates to a $281 minimum balance. So, we might conclude that new service charges are in order for all accounts under $300 minimum balance. Moreover, we could conclude that this increase in service charge should be in the neighborhood of $3.00 to $4.00 per month if all costs are to be recovered.

Service Charges Related To Activity

It is interesting to note in our example that while somewhat larger losses are associated with higher checkwriting activity, the range in total annual operating costs is relatively small — a high of $86.70 and a low of $71.64. On a monthly basis this range would be $7.23 to $5.97.

This suggests that most consumers tend to write roughly the same number of checks each month, approximately 15 to 20.

Consumer research conducted by the consulting firm of Whittle, Raddon, Motley & Hanks, Inc. has shown that consumers overwhelmingly prefer flat fee service charges, if they must be imposed. In fact, most people would prefer to pay a flat fee each month than to pay the "dime-a-time" approach, even if the latter produced substantially lower net charges!

Consequently, profit seeking bankers often elect to impose a flat monthly fee for a "base level" (say 15 to 20 checks) of monthly service.

Base Fee

Generally, you should set your "base fee" so that it reflects the average activity of your account base as a whole. For example, if your account base exhibits average activity of 16 checks, then your base fee might be:

$$(16 \times \$.21) + \$3.24 = \$6.60$$
$$\text{where}$$

(Activity × Loaded Activity Cost) + Account Maintenance = Base Fee

Or, for simplicity, you may prefer to round this base fee to $6.00 or $7.00. The important thing in setting your base fee is that it be high enough to reflect your account base activity, and low enough to satisfy competitive conditions.

Table 1.8 illustrated the potential for reducing checking deficits by cross-selling savings. If your checking fee is low, you'll see that even 100% cross-sell of savings will not bring you out of the hole.

Table 1.11 extrapolates the data to reflect the realities of your entire checking base.

TABLE 1.11   Format for Calculating Profitability of Checking Base

Average Balance	Checking #	Checking Net Income	Savings #	Savings Net Income	Core Deposit Net Income
0–100					
101–200					
201–300					
301–400					
401–500					
501–600					
601–999					
1,000+					
TOTAL					

Excess Activity Fee

The "base fee" method above assures account base profitability, but you'll have customers who'll write more checks than your base fee considered. You may want to charge them an excess activity fee of $.15 to $.20 per check for checks in excess of your base fee plan.

This analysis has resulted in an implicitly recommended pricing structure, and it's one that is actually quite simple.

The structure is a minimum balance, base fee plan with an excess usage feature.

TABLE 1.12   Minimum Balance Base Fee Plan

Minimum Monthly Checking Balance	Monthly Fee For Basic Service
$0–$300	$6.00*
Over $300	No Charge

Discount For Savings:
To avoid all service charges, simply maintain $3,000 in your savings account.

*Basic service includes 20 checks. Additional checks written will be charged an excess usage fee of $.20 per check.

This plan has excellent features; and as we'll see when combined with a discount for savings, it is, in our opinion, one of the best structures for pricing checking accounts. But before we finalize this conclusion, let's examine some alternatives and other factors influencing pricing structure and strategy.

PRICING STRATEGY AND STRUCTURE

Microeconomic theorists will tell you that costs are irrelevant in the determination of price. The market determines the price, they will say, and you can decide only whether you choose to compete at that price.

While this may be true in a *theoretically* purely competitive market, there are a number of reasons why it has only limited application to checking account pricing.

First and foremost, checking accounts are a convenience-dominated service. The economist's model assumes that consumers can choose from among totally homogeneous offerings, and that as a result, they'll differentiate only on the basis of price. Checking accounts, while functionally similar among competitors, are *not* homogeneous from the customer's point of view because of the need to visit the bank from time to time to make deposits, cash checks, etc. Ironically, the product itself, in the case of checking accounts, is much less important than its method of distribution and convenient availability.

Simply put, people will pay for convenience. Just as some stores can get away with higher prices because they are more convenient for some people, banks can too, if they are more convenient.

This is the overriding reason why checking accounts are less subject to the universal law of supply and demand than other products which are distributed through common outlets. But there are other reasons.

Another reason that one bank can charge a higher price than another if the current base fee is below breakeven (e.g., $6.00 under $300 minimum), is that it can afford to lose some customers. As we'll see later in this chapter, the percent you'll lose is within a very predictable range and if done properly can be confined to low balance accounts. You can actually make more money by losing these customers. You see, another difference between checking pricing and price theory, in general, is the fact that we can offer the fee/balance trade-off. In other words, since consumers perceive a checking price as a fee/balance trade-off, and some keep high balances while others keep low balances, this trade-off can be engineered to ensure that the customers lost are the unprofitable ones. Banks can offer different ways to pay which, if structured properly, ensure that they give the best deal to the most desirable customers.

Packaged goods marketing cannot do this. All potential customers must make their purchase decision on the basis of the product's singular price as it sits there on the shelf right next to its competitors.

Market Research

There are other peculiarities related to how consumers view banks which will influence your pricing strategy and structure. The consulting firm of Whittle, Raddon, Motley & Hanks, Inc. has done many customer studies of attitudes toward banking and the following findings seem quite universal.

- People are generally more sensitive to the way banks charge than to the amount. The term "way" is generally taken to mean the *communication* of a pricing structure. Simplicity is preferred.
- *Free Checking* or some other product attribute is usually far down the list of reasons given for selecting a bank. In an urban market, convenience is most important; in a rural market, a bank's employees and its reputation are most important.
- People do *not* generally "shop" banks for checking prices. (They do shop for CD rates, mortgage rates, etc. These are not convenience-dominated services.) The exception to this is in college towns where a very well educated market spends more time choosing a bank.
- Rarely does a person change banking relationships because of price increases, particularly if they are communicated properly to the customer. The percentage in any market who will switch are the 3% to 12% for whom convenience is less important or essentially equal.
- People call the bank where they keep their checking account their *primary* bank, but they are likely to have a savings account elsewhere.
- If encouraged to open a savings account at a bank (e.g., through a premium offer), people will open it for two or three times the minimum balance requirement.
- Among people evaluating packaged plans, their preferred methods of paying are, in order of preference:
  1. Minimum savings balance
  2. Flat fee
  3. Minimum checking balance

Price Sensitivity of Demand

Price sensitivity (or price elasticity of demand) is a very important concept in pricing. In fact, it is the *key* to determining whether a particular increase or decrease in price is a good strategy. In a competitive situation, it is assumed that as one competitor raises (or lowers) prices, customers will react by changing where they do business. But if a contemplated increase in price produces greater incremental revenues from those customers who remain than it loses from those customers who leave, then it is a good pricing decision. This kind of demand/price relationship is called *price insensitive* or *price inelastic*. Under such a situation, potential customers are relatively insensitive to price changes. As prices go up, profits go up. As prices go down, profits go down.

If a contemplated increase in price chases so many customers away that more revenue is lost than gained, the demand/price relationship is said to be *price sensitive* or *price elastic*. Under such situations, potential customers are relatively sensitive to price changes, and as prices go up, profits usually go down (unless competitors follow suit).

Example: Generally, the demand for salt is considered *price inelastic*. As the price goes up, people will still consume roughly the same quantities of salt. This is not true of electronic calculators. As we have seen, as prices for calculators began to fall from several hundred dollars to several dollars, significantly larger quantities were purchased.

Factors Influencing Price Sensitivity in Banking

There are a number of factors that influence the price sensitivity of a particular firm's product. Generally speaking, though, the two most important factors are:

- *The availability of substitute products.* If many equally convenient competitors offer the same product or service, that particular product or service will tend to be price sensitive.
- *The importance of the product's price.* If the product's price is rather insignificant relative to the consumer's total expenditures, the product or service will tend to

be relatively price insensitive (e.g., chewing gum, newspapers, etc.).

Banking services (particularly checking accounts) are influenced by both of these factors. Checking accounts from competitive institutions are usually nearly identical in the minds of consumers (though convenience certainly varies), while the overall price is *not* significant to most consumers relative to other expenditures.

It is difficult to determine the precise degree of price sensitivity you are likely to face, but there are a number of guidelines that can help your estimation. As you consider these factors, remember that each particular bank has a specific and different combination of factors influencing *its own* price sensitivity. Among the factors to be considered in estimating possible price sensitivity are:

- *Convenience*
  Convenience is probably the single most important determinant of price sensitivity. The greater the degree of banking convenience as measured by branching, ATMs, point of sale banking systems, etc., or the greater the number of competitors, the more sensitive potential customers will be to price.

- *Population Turnover*
  The greater the turnover in your market's population, the more often your bank's prices are being evaluated in a comparative sense. The more your prices are evaluated, the greater the degree of price sensitivity you are likely to face.

- *Competitive Pricing History*
  In most markets, the prices of checking accounts (or other services) tend to gravitate toward some common market price. Frequently any change will be quickly matched as competitors pursue fairly independent pricing policies. Generally, the more quickly prices gravitate toward a market price, the greater the prevalence of market price sensitivity.

- *Product Differentiation*
  The greater the difference between competitors' products, the less price sensitivity each will face. For each competitor who comes up with a preferred difference in a product, the likelihood of price sensitivity decreases. For example, for a while in some markets the "packaged account" (where customers pay a flat fee for checking plus an accumulation of other services such as insurance or travelers checks) represented a preferred difference, and it faced little price sensitivity.

- *Market Segmentation*
  The greater the ability of one institution to carve out a niche in the market for itself, (e.g., senior citizens, the blue collar segment, executives, farmers) the lesser the degree of price sensitivity it will face. Consumer finance companies are excellent examples of this phenomenon. They have positioned themselves as places for the little guy and have been able to charge higher prices because these people feel wanted there. At the other extreme, Morgan Guaranty in New York and the Northern Trust Company in Chicago have had similar successes.

- *Income*
  The lower the general level of personal income in a market, the more important the prices of consumer products become and the greater the price sensitivity that will prevail. In markets where people have relatively low incomes, $4.00 or $5.00 a month for a checking account may seem extravagant, while in more affluent settings this sum may be insignificant. Offsetting this factor to some degree is the higher level of general sensitivity among the affluent to matters pertaining to finance.

- *Marketing of Other Products*
  Banks successful in cross-selling other banking services to checking customers usually face much less price

sensitivity among current customers. Banks that successfully link together various services and price them as a package usually face less price sensitivity. NOTE: The key word in this statement is *successfully*. If the benefits of the package are not apparent, the issue of price will be more important.

- *Reputation/Image*
  Consumer studies in most markets indicate that the two reasons most consumers cited for selecting a primary bank are:

  - Convenience
  - Reputation/Image/Word of mouth

  Products and services usually rank third. If your bank is the leader in your market, you probably face less price sensitivity.

While there may be other factors influencing the price sensitivity you are likely to face, this list will serve as a useful starting point. As you consider these and other factors, remember that the *relative* importance of the variables will change depending upon the size of the market. Some things are fairly characteristic.

Most Important Price Sensitivity Factors

- Small Markets (Population under 30,000)
  Reputation/Image/Word of mouth
  Income level
  Convenience

- Middle-Sized Markets (30,000 to 100,000)
  Convenience
  Reputation/Image
  Degree of product differentiation

- Large Markets (Over 100,000)

  Convenience (less important in statewide branching states since all competitors are usually equally convenient).

- Degree of Product Differentiation or Market Segmentation
- Reputation/Image

Evaluating Price Sensitivity in Your Market

Each banking market has a particular set of conditions influencing the price sensitivity likely to be encountered by each competitor. You should try to evaluate whether your market is generally price sensitive or not. The following questionnaire may be helpful in this rather subjective effort.

PRICE SENSITIVITY SCORE CARD

Scoring Your Market Price Sensitivity

Convenience

Which of the following statements best describes the general availability of banking alternatives as measured by branches, competitors, electronic banking, or other services?

☐ *Many competitors, equally convenient.* A person does not have to go very far from our facility to find an alternative.

Score 1

☐ *Moderate competitive alternatives, somewhat convenient.* While there are alternatives, for many we are measurably more convenient.

Score 2

☐ *Few competitors.* For many we are significantly more convenient.

Score 3

Score _____

Population Turnover

Which of the following best describes the population turnover in your market during a year?

☐ 20% or more of population is new to area within one year.

Score 1

☐ 10% to 20% of population is new.

Score 2

☐ Less than 10% is new.

Score 3

Score _____

Competitive Pricing History

Which of the following statements best describes the prices, pricing strategies, and pricing structure of the competitors in your market?

☐ Nearly identical prices and pricing structure. When one changes, the others usually follow.

Score 1

☐ Some similarities, some differences

Score 2

☐ Competitors follow fairly independent pricing strategies

Score 3

Score _____

Product Differentiation

Which of the following best describes the degree of competitive product differentiation not based on location which has occurred in your market?

☐ Nearly all competitors' products are the same. No attempt has been made to package or add features.

Score 1

☐ Some of the competitors are attempting to promote differences in their services.

Score 2

☐ Most competitors are strongly promoting product differences

Score 3

Score _____

Market Segmentation

Which of the following best describes the extent to which competitors target their marketing programs to specific segments of the market, such as farmers, blue collar workers, senior citizens, or executives?

☐ Few of the competitors have singled out particular segments.

Score 1

☐ There is some of this.

Score 2

☐ Most of the institutions are associated with one segment or the other.

Score 3

Score _____

Income

Which of the following best describes the general income level of your market?

☐ Tending toward lower.

Score 1

☐ Middle income.

Score 2

☐ Tending toward higher.

Score 3

Score _____

Cross-Selling

Which of the following statements best describes the degree of multiple usage of financial institutions in your market?

☐ People generally use two or three financial institutions.

Score 1

☐ People may use two, but generally only use one.

Score 2

☐ People only use one financial institution.

Score 3

Score _____

Reputation/Image

Which of the following best describes the extent to which competitors have definitive reputations or images in your market?

☐ No bank really has a clear cut image; they are all seen as about the same.

Score 1

☐ The banks have images, but they are rather weak.

Score 2

☐ The banks have clear cut images and reputations.

Score 3

Score _____

Total Score _____

Score Your Market

You are now ready to *estimate* the price sensitivity in your market. If you have scored your market according to our questionnaire, you may use the following guidelines.

Questionnaire Score	Checking Accounts
Score of 8	*Be Careful* — a percentage increase in price may result in an equal percent decrease in volume.
Score of 8 to 14	*Raise prices* a little bit at a time; the percentage decrease in volume should be less than the percentage increase in price.
Score of 14 to 21	*Raise prices.* Your change in volume should be insignificant relative to your change in price.
Score of over 21	*Prices should be set in connection with a strategy* to discourage entry into your market of more competitors.

As you study this questionnaire and the factors it describes, remember that the relative importance of the factors will change in each market. Additionally, each competitor will have specific strengths and/or weaknesses regarding some of the important factors. To get a more refined view of the impact of price sensitivity on your pricing strategy, you should now score the individual competitors in your market on these more important factors where differences between institutions exist (e.g., convenience and product differentiation).

Scoring Individual Institution Price Sensitivity

Some of the factors described above pertain to your market, while others pertain to specific characteristics of competitive financial institutions. After you have used the overall list to evaluate your market's general price sensitivity, you will want to score each competitor's specific attributes. To make this score meaningful, each attribute must be subjectively weighed in terms of its overall importance in your market. Table 1.13 is an example and a suggested format for evaluating price sensitivity.

TABLE 1.13   Price Sensitivity Evaluation Form (Personal Checking Accounts)

		Competitors							
Factor	Score	1st City		2nd National		Bank & Trust		ABC Bank	
		Score	Weight*	Score	Weight	Score	Weight	Score	Weight
Locations	25	10	250	7	175	9	225	6	150
Reputation	20	9	180	9	180	10	200	8	160
Product Differences	15	7	105	7	105	7	105	10	150
Hours of Operation	10	7	70	7	70	7	70	10	100
Segmented Market	5	4	20	4	20	5	25	6	30
Total Score			625		550		625		590

*Weight refers to the "factor score" × the "competitor score" on that factor. Individual bank scores determined on a 1 to 10 basis.

In this example, each of the important factors influencing price sensitivity was weighed for overall importance. Each was given a score between 0 and 25. Since convenient location was determined to be most important, it was given the highest score. Other scores were determined relative to this score. Next, each bank score on each factor was determined. This can be done either subjectively or through external market research. Scores given were between 0 and 10, with 10 being highest. While a bank could earn a 10, it was not necessary to award one bank a 10 if none qualified for this rank. Let's examine the numbers behind our ratings in the example.

- *Locations*
  This market has a population of about 80,000, so locational convenience was deemed most important. First City is the largest bank and has five branches. Bank & Trust has four, Second National has three, and ABC has only two.

- *Reputation*
  While Bank & Trust is slightly smaller than First City, it enjoyed a better reputation. Market research studies always put it first in overall reputation. First City and Second National both possess good reputations, but fall slightly behind Bank & Trust. ABC Bank is a relatively new suburban bank. Its reputation is improving, but it is not seen by consumers to possess the professionalism of the larger banks.

- *Product Differences*
  ABC Bank offers a $5.00 per month package account as well as the regular $300.00 minimum balance checking plan. The other banks offer only the minimum balance plan. The ABC Bank has generally led the market with new services.

- *Hours of Operation*
  The ABC Bank is open from 9:00 a.m. to 5:00 p.m. every day and until 7:00 p.m. in the drive-ins just like

the other banks, but it also opens on Saturday from 9:00 a.m. to 2:00 p.m.

- *Market Segmentation*
  While segmentation is not strong in this market, ABC has tried to position itself as innovative to appeal to the "young, aware" market. Bank & Trust has always been perceived as the "status bank," while First City and Second National have done little to segment the market.

Given this analysis, one might draw the following conclusions:

- First City and Bank & Trust are likely to face the least amount of price sensitivity. First City will face less because of its superior convenience and Bank & Trust less because of its image and segmented market.
- ABC Bank is likely to face some price sensitivity because of convenience disadvantages. It has offset this through a program of product differentiation and extended hours.
- Second National will probably face the most price sensitivity. It is not the most convenient place to bank and has done little in the way of product differentiations or market segmentation to offset this disadvantage.

Pricing Strategy

By now you can see that factors influencing a bank's best checking price level differ according to inherent strengths and weaknesses. Depending upon the particular combination of factors, each bank is likely to have a best price. It is very difficult to determine the absolute best price. But it is fairly easy to determine whether your basic strategy should be to price above or below the market. Following are some factors that will influence this decision.

- *Market Price*
  If the prevailing market price is above breakeven, further increases will tend to export profitable business, while if the market price is below breakeven (as is usually the case), well-structured prices can surgically remove unprofitable accounts or force them to cover their costs.

- *Your Bank's Size and Preeminence*
  If your bank is the largest and most preeminent bank in the market, your strategy should be to continually differentiate your offering so exact price comparisons cannot be made. If your bank is smaller, you may have no alternative but to use price aggressively to attract more distant customers. But since many of your existing customers chose your convenience, it is best to do this on a segmented basis (i.e., saver's club or senior citizens club).

- *Earnings Characteristics*
  If your bank is a good earner with high yields and low operating costs, you may be able to afford to undercut the market price and attract marginally profitable business. Rarely, however, does this argue for free checking, since the incremental costs are so high relative to *deposits* (not customers) attracted.

  If your bank needs to improve earnings, a breakeven price can virtually assure the elimination of unprofitable business. If you're already at breakeven, further increases need to be evaluated carefully (see section on testing price increases).

- *Cross-Sell*
  As a commercial bank, you probably enjoy the advantage of being your checking customer's primary or most important financial institution. But ironically, it is also highly probable that a majority of these customers keep their largest savings balance elsewhere. As the distinc-

tion between classes of financial institutions diminishes, it is critical that you develop a way to attract all of your customers' deposit business. Pricing checking accounts to encourage savings balances is a helpful way to begin.

Alternate Price Structures

By price structure, we are referring to the way in which banks charge for checking accounts. Consumer studies indicate that people are usually as sensitive to how banks charge for services as they are to how much they charge.

There are many pricing approaches, but today there are basically seven pricing structures in common use. Let us consider each one and its inherent strengths and weaknesses.

1. Metered Plan (per check charge)
    Under this plan, a customer is charged a fee for each check written, plus a monthly maintenance fee. Sometimes credit is given for balances maintained.

    Example
    $3.00 per month
    $.10 per check
    $.05 per $100 credit per month

    Strengths
    Equitable
    Matches activity in the account to actual costs
    Discourages excess activity
    Is easily justified to the customers

    Weaknesses
    Consumers find it confusing
    Has budget plan connotation
    There is no inherent cross-selling opportunity

2. Minimum Balance Plan
    Under this plan, a customer is not charged as long as
    his checking account balance does not go below an
    established minimum. If the balance falls below the
    minimum, a fee (usually a flat fee) is assessed.

    Example
    $300.00 minimum balance
    $5.00 charge if balance falls below $300 during
    month

    Strengths
    Simple to administer, easy to understand
    Encourages higher balances among low balance
        accounts

    Weaknesses
    Encourages excess activity
    Minimum balances are usually lower than break-
        even
    Price is highly visible and easy to compare
    Minimum balances may result in inequities if cus-
        tomer's average balance during month is high
    Some banks have established minimums and/or
        averages, but this often causes confusion
    No inherent cross-selling opportunity

3. Flat Monthly Fee
    Some banks simply charge a flat monthly fee for check-
    ing privileges.

    Example
    $5.00 per month

    Strengths
    Simple to administer, easy to understand

    Weaknesses
    Discourages balances
    Encourages activity
    Fee not necessarily related to costs
    No inherent cross-selling opportunity

4. Combination Balance/Fee (3/2/1 Plans)
    Under this arrangement graduated minimum balances
    have corresponding graduated fees.

    Example
    $100.00 minimum balance pays $5.00 per month
    $200.00 minimum balance pays $4.00 per month
    $300.00 minimum balance pays $2.00 per month
    Over $300.00 minimum pays nothing

    There are many variations to this plan such as:
    A. 4,3,2
    B. 5,3,1
    C. 4,3,2,1

    Strengths
    Encourages balances
    Variable price relates to variable value of deposits
    Easy to explain
    Easy to understand
    Easy to administer

    Weaknesses
    Variations in activity are not considered
    No inherent cross-selling opportunity

5. Free Checking
    Many banks combine free checking with higher prices
    on overdrafts, NSFs, or other auxiliary services.

    Example
    No service charges, no minimum balances
    $15.00 per overdraft

    Strengths
    Highly promotable, consumers feel entitled to free
        checking
    Shifts some of the cost burden to those who are often
        too embarrassed to complain

    Weaknesses
    Greatest appeal among least profitable segments
    Overdrafts themselves are quite costly

Places cost burden on borrowing/high balance customers

Discourages balances/increases activity

Creates high production costs

6. Package Account or Club Account

Under this plan, a customer pays one flat fee per month and gets a variety of services. Many banks use this service to combat or move away from free checking, since the perceived value of the package can be made to appear "better than free." In pricing Club Accounts, one should always remember the costs of the free services. Generally, the Club should be priced at least one or two dollars more than the maximum on the regular checking account structure.

Example (Club Account)
$6.00/month gets customer:
   free checking
   insurance
   reduced rate loans
   free safe deposit box
   free travelers checks
   overdraft protection

Strengths
Generates fee income
Can compete with free checking
Cross-sells
Is promotable

Weaknesses
Encourages activity
Discourages balances

Related Regular Checking

Minimum Monthly Balance	*Fee*
$0–400	$5.00
+$400	No Charge

7. Package Tied to Savings
    This plan is an adapted version of the fee package plan,
    where the customer earns the package as a result of a
    minimum balance savings plan.

    Example
    $2,000 in savings earns:
        no charge checking
        reduced rate loans

    Strengths
    Good cross-selling; builds savings accounts
    Simple; good customer acceptance

    Weaknesses
    Not related to activity costs
    Requires more sophisticated data processing
    capability

A Word About Earnings Credit on Balances

Many banks offer customers an earnings credit on balances each
month to offset activity costs. This significantly reduces the profitability of the low balance accounts in aggregate, because the credit
shelters potential fee income. And this fee income shelter is usually
relatively insignificant for low balance customers individually.

Example:		
	10¢	Per check
	$3.00	Maintenance
	15	Checks
	5%	Earnings credit
	$100.00	Average balance
Activity cost		$4.50
Earnings credit (.05/12 × $100)		$ .41
Net fee		$4.09

Because of the difficult manner in which this credit is computed,
the typical low balance customer places very little value on it. In fact,

as we've already seen, consumers are more sensitive to simplicity. (Studies show that many people would rather pay $5.00 flat fee than $4.09 if the latter were computed in a difficult way.) And low balance customers especially are concerned about not being overdrawn, so certain knowledge of balance levels becomes very important. Consequently, the $.41 per month means very little (it can even be a nuisance) to low balance customers. But it can shelter potential fee income. Assuming you have 5,000 such accounts, the lost fee income is $24,600 per year!

Developing Your Price

The previous analysis and commentary should put you in good position to develop your checking account price structure. I'd like to offer a recommended structure, which you can modify to accommodate your particular situation.

Before I offer this, however, it should be put within the appropriate regulatory context. It is quite clear that the regulatory distinction between various types of financial institutions is lessening. Both commercial banks and thrifts can offer interest bearing transaction accounts (i.e., NOWs). This brings up two questions:

1. Since NOWs and Super NOWs are legal, should checking still be offered?
2. What structure should the checking account fee take?

The answer to number 1 is yes. NOW accounts, as we'll see in a later chapter, are very costly and should be priced accordingly and targeted at the high balance segment of the market. This does not hold for mutual savings banks in New York State who are required by law to offer free checking accounts, but may charge for NOW Accounts.

It is important to understand at this point that from the consumer's view, a NOW account is a checking account that pays interest, not a savings account upon which checks may be written. People generally do *not* combine checking and savings balances in their new NOW account, even though it and a savings account both earn about the same rate. The interest rate is an attractive feature of the NOW, but people still segregate, both psychologically and in actuality, their "transaction" balances from their "rainy day" balances.

As we'll see, a NOW account is a checking product for high balance people. It should be priced with this in mind. And the checking account should still be positioned as the best deal for the average man in the street.

Given this, the objectives to be served by your pricing structure are:

- Recover all activity costs at every balance level
- Attract balances — both checking and savings
- Be simple to explain and understand

Recommended Structure

It can be argued that you should set a base fee at approximately your cost. For example, if your average activity is 16 checks, then your base fee would be $6.00 ($16 \times \$.21 + \$3.24 = \$6.60$). This is reduced from $6.60 to $6.00 for two reasons: 1) it is simpler to understand; and, 2) even low balances carry some investment value (e.g., $50 \times .078/12 = \$.33$).

This base fee, then, should be reduced for checking or savings balances according to a schedule like the one in Table 1.14.

TABLE 1.14   Schedule for Reducing Checking Fees for Savings Balance.

Minimum Checking Balance	Minimum Savings Balance				
	0–$1,000	$1,001–$1,500	$1,501–$2,000	$2,001–$2,500	+$2,500
$0–$100	$6	$4	$3	$2	FREE
$101–$200	$5	$3	$2	FREE	FREE
$201–$300	$4	$2	FREE	FREE	FREE
$301–$400	$3	FREE	FREE	FREE	FREE
+$400	FREE	FREE	FREE	FREE	FREE

While theoretically accurate, this plan can appear confusing to customers. It might be preferable to smooth off the rough edges by offering a simplified version.

TABLE 1.15 Simplified Version of Schedule for Reducing Checking or Savings Balance.

Minimum Checking Balance	Minimum Savings Balance	
	$0–$3,000	Over $3,000
$0–$400	$6	FREE
+$400	FREE	FREE

Such a plan encourages balances with a built-in preference for savings and investment balances, where depository institutions are most vulnerable. It also assures that low balance customers' costs are covered.

Such a plan would be beneficial to both the consumer and the bank.

From the bank's viewpoint, it would waive $72.00 in potential service charges for as little as $3,000 in savings. Recognizing that $673 of this $3,000 is needed to cover savings activity costs, the remainder ($2,327) could be invested at a net margin of 4.49% to produce $104 per year. And since the original $72.00 annual fee was set to approximate costs, these customers who elect to pay with savings balances are actually somewhat more profitable.

This approach also has a distinct consumer advantage. The consumer earns interest on the $3,000 in savings and avoids $72.00 in charges.

Test Various Prices

Now you are ready to test the impact that various checking prices will have on your income. This process integrates the relatively definite cost/revenue data with projected "guestimates" about how changes in price might effect total volume.

Example

To better examine these dynamics, let us consider an example. Suppose we are talking about a personal checking account product structured as a "fee" package. The current fee is $4.00 per month and the customer is given no charge checking plus other services. Let us consider what will happen to volume, costs, and profits as prices change.

- Average monthly balance = $500.00. It is estimated that this will not change as a result of price changes, though some accounts may leave.
- Checking costs. Average activity of 16 checks per month. Cost per check is $.21 plus $3.24 maintenance cost. It is also estimated that the existing capacity will accommodate any reasonable change in volume.
- The earnings credit on checking balances is 7.78%.
- The number of checking accounts is currently $10,000.

For illustrative purposes, let us assume that our analysis of this bank's market and its competitors suggest that it should face moderate price sensitivity. The current market price for personal checking accounts is $4.00 for a package including no charge checking. It is estimated by the bank's management that increases in price will result in loss of business and that decreases in price will attract new customers. Because the competitors are nearly equally convenient, decreases in price are likely to attract customers from all of the other competitors, while increases will chase people away from only one.

In other words, we feel that if we raise our price and our competitors do not follow, we will lose some accounts, and that the higher we raise our price, the more accounts we'll lose. We also think that if we lower our price and our competitors do not, we will attract some of their customers. Since there are, say, four competitors, we think that lower prices will attract many more customers than higher prices will chase away.

To quantify these relationships, unfortunately, requires some guessing. And in Table 1.16, we guess that the following relationship might prevail.

TABLE 1.16   Possible Relationship Between Price and Number of Accounts Gained or Lost.

	Price	Estimated Number of Accounts	% Gain or Loss
	$6.00	5,800	− 42%
	$5.60	8,000	− 20%
	$5.20	8,700	− 13%
	$4.80	9,200	− 8%
	$4.40	9,700	− 3%
Current Price	$4.00	10,000	0
	$3.60	11,200	+ 12%
	$3.20	12,400	+ 24%
	$2.80	15,200	+ 52%
	$2.40	18,000	+ 80%
	$2.00	20,000	+100%

To estimate the effect that these changes in volume will have on overall profitability, we simply compute total revenues (both fees and balances) and total operating costs for each anticipated new price and compare this figure with our current profit.

This is shown in Table 1.17, "Price Sensitivity Summary Example."

TABLE 1.17   Price Sensitivity Summary Example

Price		Volume		Revenue	Cost	Profit	Change in Profit From Base
+50%	$6.00	(−42%)	5,800	$ 643,220	$ 459,360	$183,860	+$106,360
+40%	$5.60	(−20%)	8,000	$ 848,800	$ 633,600	$215,200	+$136,200
+30%	$5.20	(−13%)	8,700	$ 881,310	$ 689,040	$192,270	+$115,270
+20%	$4.80	(− 8%)	9,200	$ 887,800	$ 728,640	$159,160	+$ 82,160
+10%	$4.40	(− 3%)	9,700	$ 889,490	$ 768,240	$121,250	+$ 44,250
Current	$4.00		10,000	$ 869,000[1]	$ 792,000[2]	$ 77,000	0
−10%	$3.60	(+12%)	11,200	$ 919,520	$ 887,040	$ 32,480	−$ 44,520
−20%	$3.20	(+24%)	12,400	$ 958,520	$ 982,080	($ 23,560)	−$100,560
−30%	$2.80	(+52%)	15,200	$1,102,000	$1,203,840	($101,840)	−$178,840
−40%	$2.40	(+80%)	18,800	$1,218,600	$1,425,600	($207,000)	−$284,000
−50%	$2.00	(+100%)	20,000	$1,258,000	$1,584,000	($326,000)	−$403,000

[1]Revenue is determined by adding balance related income to fee income — $389,000 balance related income ($500 × .0778 × 10,000) and $480,000 in fee income (4.00 × 12 × 10,000).
[2]Costs are determined by multiplying number of accounts by estimated activity costs — 10,000 × $6.60 × 12 = $792,000.

After studying Table 1.17 for a few minutes, a few fundamentals become clear:

1. Lower prices attract more business than higher prices lose. This is because price sensitive customers make up a portion of each bank's customer base, and lower prices pull from all of your competitors, while raising just your price chases away only your price sensitive customers.
2. Increases in volume are not always desirable. If the new price results in a situation where total costs are rising faster than total revenues, the bottom line may actually suffer as a result of this marketing "success."
3. There is usually a price beyond which the decrease in volume hurts more than the increase in revenue. In

our example, the best price is $5.60, since at $6.00 the expected loss of customers overwhelms the increase in revenues.

It is also clear that this type of analysis is based largely on estimates. Unfortunately, this must be done since there is no way to know for sure how volume will respond to price. To spread the risk of this unknown, it might be wise to involve other members of your bank's staff. Call a meeting of interested parties; lay out your scenario and fill in the blank part of the table by means of discussion or questionnaire. In this way you broaden the participation in the decision.

Please estimate the number of accounts you think you would have after one year.

Price		Volume
$6.00		_____
$5.60		_____
$5.20		_____
$4.80		_____
$4.40		_____
$4.00	Current	10,000
$3.60		_____
$3.20		_____
$2.80		_____
$2.40		_____
$2.20		_____

A Final Comment on Testing Prices

Testing alternative prices is the most important phase of the entire pricing exercise, but it cannot be done without an understanding of your bank's costs and revenues and price sensitivity.

Testing brings all the pricing aspects together, but getting to the testing stage requires some work and judgment. The following table is a sample for you to experiment with.

TABLE 1.18   Format for Testing Prices.

Price	Volume	Revenue	Cost	Profit
+50%				
+40%				
+30%				
+20%				
+10%				
Current				
−10%				
−20%				
−30%				
−40%				
−50%				

IMPLEMENTING NEW PRICES

In recent years, most banks have been adjusting their service charges on checking accounts. The consulting firm of Whittle, Raddon, Motley & Hanks, Inc. has worked with over 200 of these banks. In the process, they learned some very important guidelines you should be following when implementing your new prices.

- *Try to change price structure to accommodate new and different offer*
  If you can tell your customers that you've come up with a new way to give even greater value for deposits (i.e., discount for savings), they're much more likely to react favorably than if you say, "Gee, because of factors beyond our control we've had to raise prices."

- *Lower quality of other checking plan*
  If you've promised "free checking for life" or for some other reason cannot automatically convert everyone to your new plan, decrease the value of the old plan. Things you can do are:

  truncate checks

  charge more for check printing

  close out if overdrawn

  no automatic overdraft protection

- *Communicate with customers*
  Sometimes you'll want everyone to get your announcement at the same time. If you want to draw attention to your new price or product to either close out low balance customers or encourage greater conversion, send everyone a first-class letter at the same time.

  On the other hand, if you want to take advantage of people's innate lack of interest in your business, simply put a plain announcement in your monthly statement. You'd be surprised at how many people won't even *notice* your adjustment.

- *Carefully develop your message and format*
  When changing prices, you might ask yourself, "Should I publicize my change in price, or just change it and hope no one notices?" It is our view that basic changes in the price of a checking account should be communicated to your customers. That is, if you change any of the following factors that influence the normal price a customer is likely to pay, you are obliged to inform him.

  Minimum balance

  Per check charge

  Fee if below minimum, or under a package plan

  Account maintenance

- *Identify high balance customer*
  To minimize upsetting your high balance customers, have your data processor provide you with a list of all accounts where the average balance exceeds some profitable level, say $1,000, and hand write on each pricing announcement, "Mrs. Jones, because of your balance level, this change will not affect your account. Thank you for your business."

  Here is a list of "do's" and "don't's" which may be of help in your implementation process.

  Avoid the word "increase." Talk about a new price structure and an adjustment to your service charges.

  Suggest that the change will not affect most customers.

  Don't apologize.

  Keep your message short.

  Don't use gummed labels over the old price schedule.

  Announce in the winter or when local conditions divert attention.

  Don't wait for competitors. There is very little advantage to being last.

- *Training*
  Experience shows that people in your market who are most sensitive to your price increase ("adjustment") are your own employees. In my experience, those banks having the most difficult time with the increase are those who've communicated least with their employees. Following are some suggested guidelines to ensure that your employees are supportive of your program.

  Share analysis with them
  Take the time to show your employees just how much a checking account costs and how much money your bank is losing.

Show how the increase will benefit them.
Talk about how the increase is not only fair, but how it
will be used to improve the bank, not only as a place to
bank but also as a place to work. Talk about better
working facilities, more money for raises, and training
seminars. Some banks have even taken 10% of the
increase after one, two, or three months and distributed it to employees according to salary levels.

The CEO or some senior executive should be
involved in these meetings to show top management
support.

Allow employees to "vent steam"
Customer contact people should also meet in smaller
groups to discuss how they are going to handle objections. These sessions are excellent for role playing
when employees take turns being the grumbling customer. Employees are very enterprising in developing
responses to customer gripes.

*Admit to employees that you expect to lose some
business*
Employees feel bad when customers gripe and leave
the bank. It hurts their pride. Tell them that you expect
to lose a certain number of customers, and their job is to
keep that figure to a minimum.

*Don't imply that "low balance customers" are
undesirable*
Many of us are "low balance customers" and so are
some of your employees. Don't suggest that you don't
want their business. Rather, explain that in the evolving new world of banking, everyone is going to have to
cover his or her costs. Like any other service, banking
services have costs that need to be recovered.

Plan the timing carefully
Be sure to phase in the increase properly. This means
initiating the new price at the new accounts desk about

one month before your announcement to existing customers. Work back from your target date according to a
schedule.

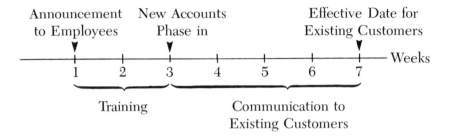

SAMPLE CUSTOMER LETTERS

Following is a compilation of repricing letters used by various banks.
Each contains some very good elements and can be combined for
your ideal letter.

Dear Customer:

   Your satisfaction with our bank has always been important to us, and top
quality service has long been our standard. In order to maintain the quality service
to which you have become accustomed, we find it necessary to adopt a new method
of pricing our Century checking accounts.
   Beginning July, 19X9, the following schedule will be in effect:

Minimum Monthly Checking Balance	Monthly Fee
$ 0–$ 99	$4
$100–$199	$3
$200–$299	$1
$300+	No Charge

   This method may result in no additional charges to the majority of our
customers because each $1,000 you maintain in your SAVINGS ACCOUNT will
give you a $1.00 discount from your monthly account service charge.

Keep $4,000 in your SAVINGS ACCOUNT and you will receive no-charge checking, regardless of your checking balance. You can see that this plan will allow you the opportunity of actually reducing your monthly service charge fees, while still allowing us the opportunity of recovering our costs.

IF YOUR CHECKING AND SAVINGS ACCOUNTS WITH US DO NOT HAVE THE SAME ACCOUNT NUMBER, IT IS IMPORTANT THAT YOU LET US KNOW SO THAT WE CAN CHANGE THEM AS THE NUMBERS MUST BE THE SAME IN ORDER FOR YOU TO GET YOUR DISCOUNT.

This is the first price adjustment National Bank has put into effect on our Century Accounts in over 20 years. During those years we faced many cost increases in processing of personal checks. We have absorbed them and not passed them on to you, our valued customer. However, checking costs have risen to a point where we can no longer absorb all of these increased costs and we are forced to adjust service charges accordingly.

If you have any questions regarding this change, or if we can be of any assistance to you, please call our Customer Service Representative, Mrs. Gladys Scott at 836-1911. She will be happy to answer all of your questions.

National Bank

According to your current balance this price adjustment will not affect your account.

Dear Customer:

Your satisfaction with our bank has always been important to us, and top quality service has long been our standard. In order to maintain the quality service to which you have become accustomed, we find it necessary to adopt a new method of pricing our Century checking accounts.

Beginning July, 19X9, the following schedule will be in effect:

Minimum Monthly Checking Balance	Monthly Fee
$ 0–$ 99	$4
$100–$199	$3
$200–$299	$1
$300+	No Charge

This method may result in no additional charges to the majority of our customers because each $1,000 you maintain in your SAVINGS ACCOUNT will give you a $1.00 discount from your monthly account service charge.

Keep $4,000 in your SAVINGS ACCOUNT and you will receive no-charge checking, regardless of your checking balance. You can see that this plan will allow you the opportunity of actually reducing your monthly service charge fees, while still allowing us the opportunity of recovering our costs.

IF YOUR CHECKING AND SAVINGS ACCOUNTS WITH US DO NOT HAVE THE SAME ACCOUNT NUMBER, IT IS IMPORTANT THAT YOU LET US KNOW SO THAT WE CAN CHANGE THEM AS THE NUMBERS MUST BE THE SAME IN ORDER FOR YOU TO GET YOUR DISCOUNT.

This is the first price adjustment National Bank has put into effect on our Century Accounts in over 20 years. During those years we faced many cost increases in processing of personal checks. We have absorbed them and not passed them on to you, our valued customer. However, checking costs have risen to a point where we can no longer absorb all of these increased costs and we are forced to adjust service charges accordingly.

If you have any questions regarding this change, or if we can be of any assistance to you, please call our Customer Service Representative, Mrs. Gladys Scott at 836-1911. She will be happy to answer all of your questions.

National Bank

Dear Customer:

Your satisfaction with our bank has always been important to us, and top quality service has long been our standard. In order to maintain the quality service to which you have become accustomed, we find it necessary to adopt a new method of pricing our Check-O-Matic accounts.

This is the first price adjustment National Bank has put into effect on Check-O-Matic Accounts in over 20 years. During those years we faced many cost increases in processing of personal checks. We have absorbed them and not passed them on to you, our valued customer. However, checking costs have risen to a point where we can no longer absorb all of these increased costs and we are forced to adjust service charges accordingly.

Beginning July 19X9, the following schedule will be in effect:

CHECK-O-MATIC ACCOUNTS

Monthly Maintenance Service Charge	Per Check Charge
$1.00	$.15

As an alternative to the CHECK-O-MATIC ACCOUNT which you now have, we invite you to consider our CENTURY CHECKING ACCOUNT which entitles you to no-charge checking if you maintain a $300 minimum balance in your CENTURY CHECKING ACCOUNT or $4,000 in a regular SAVINGS ACCOUNT. In a CENTURY CHECKING ACCOUNT you may write as many checks as you like without incurring any additional costs. Following is the price schedule of our CENTURY ACCOUNTS:

CENTURY ACCOUNTS

Minimum Monthly Checking Balance	Monthly Fee*
$ 0–$ 99	$4
$100–$199	$3
$200–$299	$1
$300+	No Charge

* For each $1,000 you maintain in your savings account you will receive a $1 discount from this monthly fee.

If you have any questions regarding this change, or if we can be of any assistance to you please call our Customer Service Representative, Mrs. Gladys Scott at 836-1911. She will be happy to answer all of your questions.

National Bank

Dear Checking Account Customer:

The _____ is pleased to announce a totally new concept in checking account service . . . a plan that lets you control the service charges you pay by offering *credits* against those charges for funds you keep in *both checking and savings accounts* with us.

NEW SMART SAVER ACCOUNT

This new plan is called the *SMART SAVER CHECKING ACCOUNT* . . . and all   checking customers (except business) will be changing to this new plan. One month from now, your statement will reflect this new method of computing service charges.

HOW WILL IT AFFECT YOU?

Good news! The balance you normally keep in your checking account suggests that you will not incur any service charges whatsoever.

But to assure that you don't, we urge you to keep your balance from going below $300 at any time. As long as you do not fall below that minimum balance, no charges will be incurred.

HERE'S HOW SMART SAVER WORKS — It's simple:

		Monthly Service Charge for Checking
1.	Keep at least $300 in your checking account at all times.	NONE
2.	Keep $200–$299 in your checking account at all times.	$1.50 fee, plus 10¢ per check written.
3.	Keep $100–$199 in your checking account at all times.	$2.00 fee, plus 10¢ per check written.
4.	Have less than $100 in your checking account during the month.	$2.50 fee, plus 10¢ per check written.

And, here's why we call this new checking account the *SMART SAVER CHECKING ACCOUNT.* For each $1,000 you maintain in a 5% StateMET Savings Account,* you will receive a $1 credit against your monthly checking account service charges. *Keep $4,000 in a StateMET Account and all activity charges will be eliminated.*

WE'LL SHOW YOU THE WAY

So you see, just by keeping your checking and/or savings accounts at certain levels, you really can control the checking service charges you pay. In fact, the discount you earn for keeping savings here more than offsets the slightly higher interest rate paid on regular savings by Savings and Loan Associations! Therefore, it just makes good sense to keep both checking and savings accounts with us.

Again, it appears that you are accustomed to keeping sufficient funds in your checking account to eliminate all service charges under the new plan. But we thought you'd like to know how this new service is designed anyhow. Please be assured that this change will not affect your Met Accounts in any other way. You will keep your same account number(s) . . . use the same printed checks you have been using . . . and receive your statements just like always.

If you have further questions about the new *SMART SAVER ACCOUNT*, stop by any Met Bank Office or call us at 229-2015 and ask for the SMART SAVER Center. We appreciate the opportunity to serve you and we hope you will always rely on us for all of your banking needs.

THE METROPOLITAN BANK

* If your savings are now in another type of savings account, or in another financial institution, ask about changing them to a StateMET Account, so you can qualify for this extra discount.

November, 19X8

TO OUR CUSTOMERS:

The _____ for some time has been able to provide its customers with no service charge checking accounts. However, because of increasing operating costs and the advent of automatic transfer service between savings and checking account, we have reluctantly decided to re-institute service charges for checking accounts. The minimal charges, which constitute our processing costs, will be as follows:

Service Charges Effective December 1, 19X8:

If you maintain a minimum balance of $300.00 or an average balance of $750.00, you will not be assessed a service charge. For those accounts that go below those amounts, a nominal charge of 10 cents per check and a monthly maintenance charge of 50 cents will be assessed.

We will continue to offer free checking accounts to our customers over 65 years of age, and to students. If you qualify under either of these categories, please make that fact known to any of our personnel.

If you have any questions concerning these changes, please contact any of our officers or employees.

Lastly, we want to take this occasion to express our thanks for the continued opportunity of serving you.

Dear Customer,

We have recently completed a study of our checking accounts and have determined that, in order to maintain our quality standard of service, we must make an adjustment in our service charge policy.

Effective March 1, 19X9, a minimum balance of $500 in the savings portion of your First Account must be maintained if you wish to continue free checking services. Should your savings balance drop beneath $500 in a given monthly statement period, a service charge of $3.00 will be assessed.

In light of this increase you may be interested to know more about our new First Account II Interest/Checking Plan. We are now able to offer you a zero-balance checking account linked with a 5% savings account that lets you keep all your money in savings, earning 5% interest, until you need it. We will automatically transfer the amount needed to cover your checks when they are presented to us for payment. Only the exact amount will be transferred. Your entire balance remains in savings earning 5% interest compounded daily and paid quarterly. The zero-balance checking privilege is free when you maintain a balance of at least $2000 in your 5% savings account.

If you are interested in this new service from us, stop by any of our Banking Centers or call. An account executive will be happy to help you.

Cordially,

Personal Banking Department

PRICING SPECIAL DEPOSIT SERVICES

Services such as NSFs (non-sufficient funds), overdrafts, stop payments, and account reconcilement research time, share a number of characteristics:

1. They are not pivotal reasons for people to choose a bank

2. Banks do not want to encourage the use of the service
3. They are used to a disproportionate extent by lower balance, less profitable customers

Given these characteristics and the trend in bank earnings in recent years, there has been an industry trend to raise these types of charges.

Generally speaking, these services should be priced to discourage the activity, rather than simply compensate the bank.

Special Service Charges (Average)

	1978	1980	1982
NSFs	$3.00	$ 8.00	$ 9.00
Overdrafts	3.00	8.00	9.00
Stop payment	1.00	3.00	3.00
Cashing non-customer checks	.50	1.00	2.00
Research time (per hour)	5.00	10.00	10.00

Source: Whittle, Raddon, Motley & Hanks — Chicago, Illinois

To the chagrin of some bankers (and the pleasure of others), these services show very little price elasticity of demand. In fact, many banks have doubled and tripled their prices in order to discourage activity; only to find that the activity did not change at all.

Check Protection

To avoid the embarrassment of being overdrawn, many banks have offered a small line of credit linked to a checking account. When a person then becomes overdrawn, a small loan of $25 to $100 is created to cover the overdraft. This concept has rarely proven profitable because the loans outstanding, generated by essentially lower balance customers, are too small to compensate the bank for the administration of this service.

Since it is now legal to allow limited transfer of funds from savings accounts to checking accounts, many banks are revising their definition of overdraft check protection from small loans to transfers from savings.

Other clever banks are selling check protection like insurance. Customers sign up for $10.00 per year, and then each overdraft is covered for a lower than normal fee.

Commercial Checking Account Pricing

There is a significant difference between a commercial checking account and a personal checking account. Commercial checking accounts tend to carry larger balances, exhibit higher activity, and are subject to greater scrutiny by their account holder.

Additionally, commercial accounts exhibit much greater variability among themselves than do personal checking accounts.

All of these factors argue for pricing the commercial checking account differently from the personal checking account; and that is what will be explored in this section.

Commercial Checking — Some Descriptive Statistics

Looking at our sampling of Functional Cost Analysis banks, we see some interesting statistics. For example in Exhibit A, we can see that larger banks tend to attract larger commercial customers.

EXHIBIT A — Size of Commercial Accounts

	Bank Size		
	$0–$50mm	$51mm–$200mm	$201mm+
Number of Accounts	881	2,011	11,036
Average Balance (Ledger)	$5,485	$8,951	$14,741

Source: Functional Cost Analysis

This is not necessarily true of personal checking accounts, where the size ranges tend to be similar regardless of bank size. This phenomena probably has a great deal to do with the lending aspect of the commercial account relationship, where bank "lending limits" (i.e., the maximum amount one bank may lend to a company) influence the corporate treasurer's selection of a bank.

Of greater importance in pricing commercial checking accounts, however, are some of the statistics in Exhibit B. Here we can see the pervasiveness of the so-called 80/20 principal. In even the smaller, retail banks, over 60% of total demand deposits are provided by the relatively few (16%) commercial type accounts.

EXHIBIT B — Commercial Checking as a % of Total DDA

	Bank Size		
	$0–$50mm	$51mm–$200mm	$201mm +
$	60%	65%	76%
Number of Accounts	16%	13%	15%
Checks Written	29%	36%	42%
Deposits Made	43%	30%	43%
Transit Items	72%	72%	98%

Source: Functional Cost Analysis

It is this banking fact-of-life that leads many commercial bankers to conclude that commercial accounts are much more desirable than personal accounts.

Before we jump to this conclusion, we should, however, look at the costs of servicing the commercial account. Exhibit B also shows that commercial accounts exhibit greater relative activity than personal accounts. For example, while commercial accounts in smaller banks ($0–$50mm) represent only 16% of the number of checking accounts, they account for 29% of the checks written, 43% of the deposits made, and 72% of the transit items processed. As one can see, the deposit function is more actively used by commercial accounts than by personal accounts. And since processing deposits is relatively costly, we need to look beyond raw dollar balances to make a true judgment concerning the desirability of commercial business vs. personal business. In theory, of course, all business is good business if it's priced to make a profit!

To effectively price a commercial account, you must look at how the activity in the account compares to the balance. As we've seen, the balances in commercial accounts are generally higher than in personal accounts, but so is the activity. For example, in Exhibit C, we can see the "typical" commercial customer (this term is less applicable to commercial customers and will promote a highly personalized pricing concept) of a middle-sized bank writes 51 checks, makes 7.3 deposits, and needs 88 transit items cleared during a month.

EXHIBIT C — Average Commercial Account Activity

	Bank Size		
	$0–$50mm	$51mm–$200mm	$201mm +
Checks Written	25	51	49
Deposits	6.5	7.3	8.2
Transit Items	44	88	138

As can be seen, the commercial checking account is more costly than the personal checking account. But perhaps more important than this is the extreme variability in activity among commercial accounts. This important fact argues for a somewhat more complicated pricing approach than that used with personal accounts. This approach seeks to quantify costs, give credit for balances, and make up any deficiency with a service charge.

EXHIBIT D — Commercial DDA Cost Profile (Monthly)

	Activity Cost	$0–$50mm	$51–$200mm	$201mm+
1.	Checks Written			
	#	25	51	49
	Unit Cost	$ .104	$ .115	$ .111
	Total Cost	$2.60	$5.87	$5.44
2.	Deposits			
	#	6.5	7.3	8.2
	Unit Cost	$ .21	$ .23	$ .22
	Total Cost	$1.38	$1.72	$1.81
3.	Transit Items			
	#	44	88	138
	Unit Cost	$ .054	$ .058	$ .059
	Total Cost	$2.36	$5.06	$8.16
4.	Account Maintenance	$2.81	$3.08	$3.02
	TOTAL ACTIVITY COST	$9.15	$15.73	$18.43

Source: Functional Cost Analysis

Commercial Balances, Float and Reserves

Before you can give credit for balances and thereby compute the service charge required (if any), you've got to know what proportion of your customer's balance is actually invested in your earnings asset portfolio.

Because commercial accounts make frequent deposits containing many transit items, much of their deposit is tied up in "float" — or uncollected funds; and, of course, some remains uninvested because of reserve requirements.

Exhibit E suggests approximately how much of your commercial account's deposit is investable. It is interesting to note that larger banks attract larger commercial customers, who make deposits with more transit items representing more float.

EXHIBIT E — Commercial Funds Invested

	Bank Size		
	$0–$50mm	*$51mm–$200mm*	*$201mm+*
% of Commercial DDA Funds Invested	78%	74%	66%
Float & Reserves	22%	26%	34%

Source: Functional Cost Analysis

Estimating Float

If your bank has a proof-of-deposit system, you do not have to estimate float; but, many banks do not. In these cases, the Functional Cost Analysis data can be helpful in developing an estimated "float factor" which you can apply to your commercial accounts.

Exhibit F presents an approach to separate float from reserves. Since your reserves are known, you can simply subtract this percentage from the FCAs figure for uninvested funds.

EXHIBIT F — Estimating Float

	Bank Size		
	$0–$50mm	*$51mm–$200mm*	*$201mm+*
% Uninvested	22%	26%	34%
% Reserve Requirement	10%	11%	12%
% Estimated Float	12%	15%	22%

Account Analysis

Because commercial accounts exhibit so much variability, the popular method of pricing is called "account analysis." As the name suggests, this method seeks to quantify the costs and balance related revenues of each account and make up any deficit through a service charge or balance requirement "carry forward."

Services Used

Commercial accounts use many and varied services, and it will be necessary to identify them and to estimate their costs and prices. A partial list of commercial services appears in Exhibit G.

EXHIBIT G — Partial List of Commercial Deposit Services

Checks Written	Incoming Transfer
Deposits Credited	Internal Transfer
Items Deposited	Outgoing Transfer
Account Maintenance	Return Item Re-submit
Stop Payment	Return Item Phone Call
Days Overdrawn	Coin Wrap
Return Item Charge Back	Special Handling

Since commercial accounts have varied needs, it is wise to "unbundle" your deposit services and have specific charges on each item.

The majority of the services used will be for the basic activity relationship — making deposits and writing checks. Here, the Functional Cost Analysis program can be helpful in establishing your prices since costs may be easily estimated.

EXHIBIT H — FCA Commercial Account Unit Costs

	Bank Size		
	$0–$50mm	$51mm–$200mm	$201mm+
Checks Written	$ .11	$ .12	$ .15
Deposits Credited	$ .23	$ .24	$ .30
Transit Items (Items Deposited)	$ .06	$ .07	$ .08
Account Maintenance	$3.11	$3.24	$4.13

The costs of other services would have to be estimated.

These activity costs, then, serve as the basis for pricing all commercial demand deposit accounts under an account analysis pricing approach. Exhibit I offers an example of an account analysis form showing the accumulation of costs for one month.

EXHIBIT I — Account Analysis Form

Account Name	Hagoth, Inc.
Account Number	24–00123
Month	October, 19X2

Costs

Service Performed	Unit Cost	Activity	Total Cost	
Checks Written	$ .17	62	$10.54	
Deposits Credited	$ .34	8	$ 2.72	
Items Deposited	$ .10	122	$12.20	
Account Maintenance	$ 4.54	1	$ 4.54	
Other Services (Specify):				
Internal Transfer	$ 2.00	2	$ 4.00	
Balance Inquiry	$ .50	8	$ 4.00	} $23.00
Wire Transfer	$15.00	1	$15.00	
TOTAL			$53.00	

Credit for Balances

In Exhibit I, Hagoth Manufacturing used $53.00 worth of services in October, 19X2. Please note that even though the term "unit cost" is used, these figures are prices and reflect a markup over cost. In this example, the markup is 40% over the FCA cost ($50 million to $200 million). It now needs to be questioned whether the balances were high enough to support this level of service usage. Or, in other words, did the bank make enough money by investing this account's deposit (after float and reserves) to cover this $53.00 cost?

To answer this question you must know the value of your customer's deposit to your bank. Conceptually, what you are doing is providing a variety of services to your customer, all of which cost you something, in exchange for deposits. You invest these deposits in such assets as loans or investments and the related earnings then help cover your costs.

Since customers' deposits have earnings value to banks, many will pass on part of that value to the customer. Let's say, for example, that a bank earns 12% on its customers' deposits. It might be well to share part of this with the customer rather than require explicit fees to pay for the services used. Most banks call this the "earnings credit" on commercial accounts. And there are a number of approaches you can use to quantify this. Each approach seeks to define a percentage rate which reflects the investment value of the deposit.

Money Market Rate

Many banks, especially larger ones, use the current month's money market rate as the earnings credit rate applicable to customers' investable balances. Since there are a variety of money market instruments from which to choose, banks often identify one (e.g., 90-Day Treasury Bills) or some composite group (e.g., commercial paper, T-Bills, federal funds).

The theory behind using this rate is that from the customer's viewpoint, maintaining bank balances to support services (and, hence, even using a bank) competes with other short term potential uses for customer's funds — principally investing in the money market.

Savings Account Rate

Some bankers take issue with this alternate use of funds theory. They believe that the appropriate earnings credit rate should be defined by the bank based upon its desire to control its overall cost of funds. Many of these banks elect a 5% to 6% earnings credit rate, since this figure reflects an attractive source of funds to the bank. These bankers believe that their customers cannot or will not elect to lower either their bank service use, or will pay in explicit fees.

Administered Earnings Credit Rate

Many banks feel that the money market rate is too visible and subject to abuse by customers, but they also recognize that a flat 5% may be competitively unrealistic. These banks elect to define their earnings credit rate using a formula.

In theory, this formula approximates the true value of the customer's deposit (perhaps less a markup for profit) to the bank. Customer deposits are invested in a variety of assets such as federal funds, T-Bills, T-Notes, and loans. Each of these provides a return to the bank. These returns may be averaged and weighted to reflect the make-up of the bank's portfolio. In the example in Exhibit J this weighted average is 10.3%. This figure is then adjusted downward to provide the bank with a profit margin and the result is a 9.2% earning credit.

EXHIBIT J — Example of Administered Earnings Credit

Asset	Current Rate	×	% Mix	=	Earnings Credit Factor
Federal Funds	13.5%	×	.10	=	.0135%
T-Bills (90 Day)	11.7%	×	.20	=	.0234%
T-Notes (1 Year)	10.5%	×	.20	=	.021 %
Avg. Loan Yield (Net)	9.0%	×	.50	=	.45 %
Expected Yield on Funds					.103 %
Less Profit Mark-Up*					.011 %
Administered Earning Credit					.092 %

$$\text{*Profit Spread Over Cost of Funds} = \frac{\text{Target Return on Avg. Assets}}{\text{Avg. Earning Assets} \div \text{Avg. Total Assets}} \div \frac{\text{Avg. Total Deposits}}{\text{Avg. Earning Assets}}$$

The advantages of the administered rate are its flexibility and its control. You can adjust it when conditions are advantageous.

If you elect to use an administered earnings credit where a profit spread is factored in, you may decide not to mark up your activity costs since to do so would raise customers' required balances to a level where they might become vulnerable to competitor initiatives.

Account Analysis Format

The analysis of activity costs and the application of the earnings credit are brought together, typically, on a monthly account analysis form such as that shown in Exhibit K.

EXHIBIT K — Account Analysis Format

Commercial Checking
Account Analysis

Account Name	Hagoth, Inc.
Account Number	24–00123
Month	October, 19X2

Costs

Service Performed	Unit Cost	Activity	Total Cost	
Checks Written	$ .17	62	$10.54	
Deposits Credited	$ .34	8	$ 2.72	
Items Deposited	$ .10	122	$12.20	
Account Maintenance	$ 4.54	1	$ 4.54	
Other Services (Specify):				
Internal Transfer	$ 2.00	2	$ 4.00	
Balance Inquiry	$ .50	8	$ 4.00	} $23.00
Wire Transfer	$15.00	1	$15.00	
TOTAL			$53.00	

EXHIBIT K — *(continued)*

Service Credit for Balances

Average Ledger Balance		6,500	
Less:			
Float	15 %		
Reserve Requirement	10 %		
Balances Supporting Credit	$ 0		
Investible Balances		4,875	
× (times) Earnings Credit: 10% (The 90-Day Treasury Bill Rate) =			
Service Credit for Balances			$40.62
Activity Deficiency (if any)			$12.38

NOTE: Rates are reflected on annual basis, but have been reduced to monthly factors in actual calculations.

As can be seen, this simple approach produces a figure called the activity deficiency, which is the service charge required to cover all activity costs. Many banks simply debit the account for this amount. Others carry it forward for a maximum of 12 months and debit the account then, if need be.

Automated vs. Manual

Of course, it is always preferable to automate the kind of information represented in the Account Analysis Form. But this may be impossible. This approach may be done manually using one or more of these guidelines:

1. All high volume accounts (e.g., chain stores).
2. One-twelfth of the accounts each month, as a sample to produce a target balance.
3. All of the accounts, yearly.

Fees Only For Special Services

To enhance profits further, some banks will offer earnings credit only against check writing and deposit activity. All other services result in a service charge, regardless of balances. An example of this approach is used in Exhibit L.

EXHIBIT L — Format Showing Fees for Special Services

Commercial Checking

Account Name _____

Account Number _____

Month _____

Activity Costs

	Unit Cost	Activity	Total Cost
Checks Written	$ .17	62	$10.54
Deposits Credited	$ .34	8	$ 2.72
Items Deposited	$ .10	122	$12.20
Account Maintenance	$ 4.54	1	$ 4.54
Total Activity Cost			$30.00

Balance Credit

Average Ledger Balance		6,500
Less:		
Float	15 %	
Reserves	10 %	
Balances Supporting Credit	0 %	
Investible Balances		4,875
× (times) Earnings Credit:		
10 % =		
Service Credit to Support Activity		$40.62
Activity Deficiency (if any)		$ 0

EXHIBIT L — *(continued)*

Service	Cost	Volume	Total Cost
Other Services (Fee)			
Internal Transfer	$ 2.00	2	$ 4.00
Balance Inquiry	$ .50	8	$ 4.00
Wire Transfers	$15.00	1	$15.00
Total			$23.00
Total Fees Due			$23.00

Profit

Profit may be added into the pricing mechanism in two ways:

1. A reduction in the earnings credit rate.
2. An addition to the "penny price" of the service; for example, charging $.17 per debit instead of the $.12 cost.

If your customer base is extremely sophisticated it may be better to reflect the markup in the penny price, since treasurers are less familiar with what this should be than they are with the earnings credit rate.

The extent to which various services should be marked up should be influenced by:

where they are available

whether or not you want to encourage the activity (e.g., overdrafts)

your current earnings and marketing strategy

Timing

Commercial customers are typically more sophisticated than retail customers and are much less influenced by convenience. Consequently, they tend to be more price sensitive. Nevertheless, there are some guidelines that will help you improve your commercial account profitability.

A good time to raise your penny prices is when your earnings credit rate is rising. This will tend to keep required balances at least at their current level, and treasurers monitoring balances may not notice the offsetting changes.

Don't back down. If a high volume account refuses to pay its way, export the earnings problem to someone less capable of handling it.

Use an Officer Call Program. Get your officers to go out and *explain* what you've done. Most customers will react favorably to your business person's orientation.

Don't Double Count

While it is beyond the scope of this book to discuss loan pricing, smart bankers always encourage compensating balances in loan pricing. If you've sacrificed rate in exchange for balances, do not count these same balances to support services! The number you reflect as "ledger balance" on your Account Analysis Form should be reduced by any loan-related compensating balance requirements.

Microcomputers

The approach described here may be beyond the capabilities of many mainframe commercial DDA systems. However, the approach may be implemented through the use of a microcomputer. Commercial customers are relatively few in number and there are a variety of software packages which can be used to implement the approach.

2

NOW Accounts — Historic Development

"Negotiable Orders of Withdrawal" from regular statement savings accounts — or NOW Accounts — were first offered by The Consumers Savings Bank in Worcester, Massachusetts. This event, which was to begin an historic evolution in banking, occured in 1972 after a lengthy court case in which the Massachusetts Supreme Court ruled that the novel negotiable order of withdrawal was functionally the same as existing permissable withdrawal methods.

Massachusetts savings banks began to offer NOW accounts immediately. And savings banks in neighboring New Hampshire quickly followed suit.

These actions brought strong protests from commercial banks, state banking regulators, and others. And while little was done in New England to discourage the spread of NOW accounts, the U.S. Congress acted in 1973 to limit the experiment in paying interest on checking, an action prohibited for over 40 years with which NOW accounts had become synonymous, to the two New England states of Massachusetts and New Hampshire.

The thought behind this legislation was that these two states would serve as a testing ground for the broadening of banking powers for thrifts and the gradual phasing out of distinctions between commercial banks and thrifts from the consumer's perspective.

The evolution of the NOW account between 1973 and 1979 in New England is worth further examination, since many insights may be gleaned about the relative importance of transaction access and the earning of interest on an account to both consumers and bankers.

THE NEW ENGLAND EXPERIENCE

In the early days NOW accounts were legal for financial institutions in two states, Massachusetts and New Hampshire. And as you might expect, the different classes of financial institutions had different objectives to serve in marketing NOW accounts.

Generally speaking, the savings banks saw NOW accounts as an opportunity to attract new customers and deposits. Commercial banks, on the other hand, saw NOW accounts as more of a threat, since in their view very little new money would be attracted while the costs associated with their existing deposit base would rise.

Consumer Attitudes and Behavior

Interestingly, implicit in both views is the notion that a NOW account, while legally a savings account, would compete for checking deposits and be viewed by consumers as an interest-bearing checking account.

This assumption proved correct. Consumers did see NOW accounts as substitutes for checking accounts. And in spite of promotion encouraging people to combine all of their deposit relationships into the new hybrid account, people viewed the NOW account as an interest-bearing checking account.

There are other interesting consumer attitudes underlying some of the early statistics showing NOW account balances at the various types of financial institutions.

EXHIBIT 2   Average NOW Balances in Massachusetts As
Influenced By Pricing

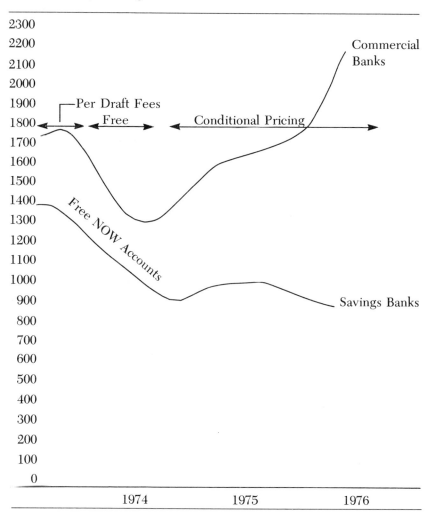

Source: Federal Reserve Bank of Boston

For example, if we look at Exhibit 2, we can see that the average
balances of NOW account users in 1974 were fairly high compared
with DDA balances. At commercial banks the average was about

$1,800, while at savings banks, it was about $1,400. Research conducted by Whittle, Raddon, Motley & Hanks, Inc. suggested that the
early adoptors of the NOW account tended to be higher balance
customers. This was somewhat unusual at the time, because banking
innovations of that period (i.e., prior to money market certificates)
tended to be transaction oriented and to appeal to lower balance
customers.

This kind of pricing prevailed in Massachusetts for only a short
time. And, while it was clear that the new service was very popular, it
was also true that only a fraction of the state's population had actually
opened NOW accounts.

Thrifts Switch Strategy

In an attempt to improve their share of the NOW account market, and
to further accelerate the movement of funds out of commercial banks,
one of the large Boston savings banks began to offer free NOW
accounts in September of 1973. The rest of the thrift industry quickly
followed suit and by 1974 the movement to NOW accounts acceler-
ated. But as can be seen in Exhibit 2, the segment of the market that
was attracted to these free NOW accounts maintained lower average
balances.

This change in pricing strategy was immediately felt by the
commercial banks, which noticed larger numbers of accounts closing.
Without studying the composition and average balances of these
closed accounts, many commercial banks decided to follow suit and
drop all NOW account service charges in mid-1974.

When the commercial banks began offering free NOW accounts,
their average NOW balance began to plummet. (See Exhibit 2.) All of
those people who were undecided about whether or not NOWs
would benefit them had all doubt removed.

Convenience is Crucial

It is important to note that the downward trajectory of the average
free NOW balance is greater in commercial banks than thrifts. This is

additional evidence to support the idea that from the consumer's perspective a NOW account is a checking account with all of the inherent dependence upon physical convenience.

In other words, a person maintaining an average DDA balance of $5,000 would have a much greater incentive (5% × $5,000 = $250) to tolerate some inconvenience than someone maintaining an average balance of $300 (5% × 300 = $15.00).

And even though the lower balance customers may not have made the calculation, their intuition told them that the inconvenience of switching just would not be worth it.

But when their own commercial bank offered free NOW accounts, all barriers were removed and new commercial bank NOW accounts began opening in large numbers.

Commercial Banks Switch Pricing Strategy Again

So successful was the move to free NOW accounts by commercial banks that they had to terminate the idea or face the prospect of converting virtually every checking account to a free NOW account.

So, toward the end of 1974 the commercial banks in Massachusetts began to impose minimum balance service charges (e.g., if your NOW account balance falls below a certain balance, you pay a fee).

As can be seen in Exhibit 2, this clearly reversed the adverse trend in average balances among commercial bank NOW accounts.

Numbers of Accounts

But we must look also at the numbers of accounts being opened. Table 2.1 shows numbers of NOW accounts by type of institution for 1974, 1975, and 1976.

When commercial banks first went to free NOW accounts in 1974 their market share in numbers of accounts jumped significantly. After they extrapolated the potential financial disaster of this marketing "success," they recanted with a minimum balance, conditional fee plan, and their growth in market share tapered off to around 34%.

TABLE 2.1   Number of NOW Accounts in Massachusetts

	Commercial Banks	Savings Banks	S&Ls and Coops	Total Mass.	Commercial Bank as % of Total
1974					
January	1,259	95,677	1,240	98,176	1%
June	7,261	132,214	12,441	151,916	5%
December	45,668	205,704	37,248	288,620	16%
1975					
June	115,232	291,035	68,924	475,191	24%
December	189,635	387,163	105,315	682,113	28%
1976					
June	293,679	473,377	132,343	899,399	33%
December	375,541	551,713	163,710	1,090,964	34%

Source: Federal Reserve Bank of Boston, *Now Account Reports*

Number vs. Dollars

So during 1975 through 1977 most commercial banks offered minimum balance NOW accounts, while savings banks offered them free.

By 1977, after two years of commercial banks offering minimum balance NOW accounts and thrifts offering free NOW accounts, the following conditions prevailed. Commercial banks had over 57% of the total NOW deposits while serving only 35% of the NOW customers. Thrifts, on the other hand, captured only 43% of the deposits, while attracting 65% of the accounts. Stated another way, the average commercial bank NOW account carried a balance of $2,236 compared with the thrift's average balance of $916.

This price competition resulted in the polarization (or segmentation) of the market for NOW accounts into the following distinct groups:

1.   Commercial bank customers whose average balances were high enough to avoid service charges

2. Commercial bank customers whose balances were too low to avoid bank service charges, but who wanted the free NOW account badly enough to switch to a thrift
3. Commercial bank customers whose balances were too low to avoid services charges, but who opened a bank NOW anyway because of the inconvenience of switching
4. Commercial bank customers who did nothing

By 1977, four years into NOW accounts, it was possible to get some idea of the relative magnitudes of these groups. By March of 1977, 1.1 million NOW accounts had opened in Massachusetts, a state with a population at that time of over 5.6 million.

If you think of the family as the consuming unit, there were about 1.9 million family units (including single person households) in Massachusetts during this period. If we are conservative and assume only one checking NOW account product per household, 1.1 million out of 1.9 million families switched from checking to NOWs in four years. This 58% is probably somewhat overstated due to multiple checking accounts per household, but it gives us some idea of the size of the group of apathetic customers who did nothing.

Among those who did open a NOW account, some stayed with their commercial bank. These accounted for 35% of the number of accounts, but 57% of the deposits. Others switched to thrifts. These accounted for 65% of the number of accounts and 43% of the deposits. The average balances were twice as high among commercial bank NOW customers. If there are any accounts who are carrying balances too low to avoid service charges, but staying with their bank and paying the charge, then we can conclude that that bank's convenience advantages are worth paying for.

Pricing Strategies Segmented the Market

In conclusion, though, we can see clearly that the competitive pricing strategies followed by thrifts and banks segmented the market. Relatively higher balance accounts stayed with their commercial bank even though they could get free NOW accounts elsewhere.

And the thrifts attracted relatively lower balance accounts with their no service charge strategy.

Early Adopters Have Higher Balances

As you ponder this data, don't jump to the obvious conclusion. There are some additional trends you need to see.

As shown in Table 2.1, both commercial bank average NOW balances ($2,236) and thrift average balances ($916) are significantly above average checking balances. In 1972 and 1975, the average balance* in New England checking accounts was:

	1972	1975
Special checking (Dime-a-time)	$271	$255
Personal minimum balance	$840	$622
Overall average	$340	$320

*Boston Federal Reserve Bank FCA data

Considering this data in light of the fact that NOW accounts grew gradually and still have not totally replaced checking accounts, one thing is clear — the early adopters of NOW accounts tend to be higher balance customers. And the longer NOW accounts were around, the greater the erosion in average balances.

This is true of virtually all new banking services which, by virtue of interest payments, appeal primarily to the higher balance segments of the market. The early adopters tend to be higher balance, more affluent customers. Then as the product matures, it appeals to successive segments of the market having lower average balances.

This erosion occurs for two reasons.

1. The early adopters are more financially sophisticated and more inclined to experiment. When they first open their NOW account, they might combine checking with some savings deposits, and keep their checking account. Eventually, though, they see how easy it is to spend and they adjust their average balances accordingly, maintaining once again that functional split between savings and checking deposits.
2. Newer, lower balance, less sophisticated customers hear about NOW accounts and begin opening them.

Should You Pay Maximum Interest?

Another issue that we'll explore later, but for which there is some evidence growing out of the New England experience, is whether or not to pay the full permissable rate of interest.

Savings banks in New Hampshire, the other state initially given NOW powers, flirted with the idea of offering NOW accounts free of service charges, but paying only 2% or 3% interest.

This pricing strategy was designed to make the NOW account more of a direct competitor to commercial bank checking accounts. This strategy failed very early and savings banks began raising the interest rates paid on NOW accounts.

In retrospect and with the advantage of market research, it is easy to see why this strategy failed.

1. There was no incentive for people to combine savings and checking deposits. In fact, there was a greater incentive to maintain separate accounts. And among those who were interest rate sensitive, the rate differ-ential only encouraged lower NOW balances. Even though a small minority of people exhibited a tendency to combine checking and savings, the early adopters in Massachusetts showed a greater tendency and this was reflected in their average balances.

EXHIBIT 3   Early Pricing Strategies and Average NOW Balances

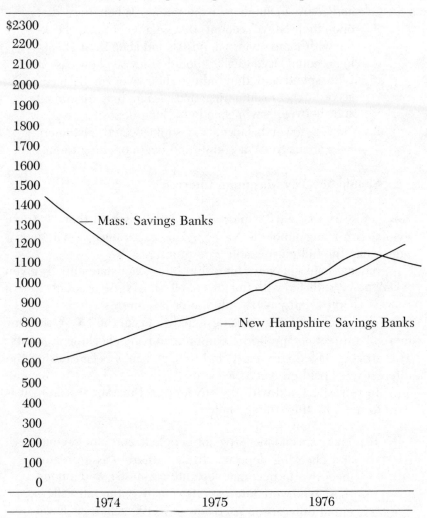

Source: Federal Reserve Bank of Boston

2. The "no service charge" feature of the New Hamp-
    shire NOW was strongly promoted and accounted for a
    high proportion of the reasons to switch. In general,
    these accounts tended to be lower balance accounts.

It did not take the New Hampshire savings bankers long to see the error of their initial strategy and in 1974 they began to raise the interest rates paid. By 1975 virtually all were paying the maximum.

Lower Profitability Starts Trend Toward Pricing

Another trend that gave impetus to the New Hampshire savings bankers' early move toward repricing the NOW account were the costs. Savings bankers learned that with the new NOW customers came their operating costs. And that these costs, given the higher activity of the NOW account, were in the $50.00 to $60.00 per year range based upon Functional Cost Analysis studies done during the mid-1970s. Even with the higher interest margin produced by lower interest costs (7% yield − 3% = 4% margin), the breakeven average balance per NOW account was in the $1200 to $1500 range. This simply did not square with the existing $500 to $600 average balance accounts. And New Hampshire savings bankers began to search for ways to improve profitability.

The Evolution Toward A Market Price

As we've seen, the various classes of competitors in New England began marketing NOW accounts with widely divergent objectives and pricing strategies. Commercial banks sought to discourage the NOW account by offering very restrictive pricing. The savings banks generally sought to improve market share by offering free or near-free NOWs.

As time wore on, the commercial banks lowered prices and gradually imposed conditional (fee/balance) pricing in an attempt first to stop account erosion, then to confine that erosion to the smaller accounts.

Savings banks, on the other hand, at first were pleased with the apparent success of the NOW account. Then they began to recognize that because of their pricing, many of the accounts carried more costs than earnings. So they began to search for ways to get compensation for the costs, and attract the higher balance customers who were staying with their commercial banks because of the condition (fee/balance) pricing.

As this situation matured, a market price began to emerge. The fee/balance trade-off seemed to work best in achieving the dual goals of recovering costs and attracting profitable customers. And by 1982, the most common type of NOW accounts required a minimum balance of between $300 and $1500 to avoid services charges. And if a customer's balance falls below the required minimum, a service charge is imposed. This charge is, in some cases, a flat fee of, say, $4.00 or $5.00. And in other cases it is a per item charge, such as $.15 per draft, plus a monthly maintenance fee.

The New England Experience — In Conclusion

Fortunately for the rest of the country, Congress did elect to try out the NOW account on a regional basis. We learned a lot about customer's attitudes toward NOW accounts; and we learned a lot about the costs of getting into and making money in the transaction account business.

Before we turn our attention to the specifics of NOW account pricing, it's helpful to review what the New England experience taught us, since many of the principles may be equally applicable to other types of banking products in the future.

The New England Experience — What We Learned

1. NOW Accounts are perceived as checking accounts that pay interest; not as savings accounts.
2. Generally speaking, only a small minority of people will combine savings and checking balances into a NOW account or any other transaction account which they plan to use frequently to buy things or pay bills. And even this tendency erodes as people begin to see that a NOW account functions as a checking account. People see checking accounts and NOW accounts as spending mechanisms; and savings accounts, CDs,

etc., as saving or investing mechanisms. Interestingly, with the development of "checkable" money market mutual funds in the early 1980s, people still maintain separate checking or NOW Accounts, since according to the Investment Company Institute the average money fund customer writes only two drafts per year!

3. The early adopters of NOW accounts are typically more financially sophisticated and carry higher balances. As NOW accounts become more widely accepted, average balances market-wide begin to fall.

4. Pricing above your competitor on a fee/balance plan will ensure higher average balances for you; and the loss of some accounts — mostly low balance — to your competitor.

5. Consumers are more inclined to open a NOW account where they have a checking account; and will generally endure a slightly higher price rather than suffer the inconvenience of switching suppliers.

6. Consumers would much rather have a NOW account paying the maximum interest rate and requiring a service charge than one carrying a lower rate but requiring no charge.

> **Comment:** This confirms the principle that since people cannot easily compute the dollar value of interest, they are inclined to overestimate its true value!

7. NOW accounts do not necessarily replace checking accounts. Many people have so little money in checking that they are unwilling to incur any inconvenience in opening a new account. The breakeven point on a NOW account (in average balances) is so high that many, if not a majority, are better off with a rationally priced checking account as opposed to a rationally priced NOW.

8. The term "NOW Account," while confusing at first, gradually became synonymous with the product — interest-bearing checking. Some banks call their product "NOW Checking" or something similar, but virtually all banks use the term NOW somewhere in their product name.

PRICING THE NOW ACCOUNT

As I mention throughout this book, in an industry like banking, costs are very important in setting prices. This is not to say that costs *determine* prices, since we are free to set any price we want. But in an industry like ours with historically poor earnings (compared to other industries) and further pressures to erode the historic source of earnings (i.e., the net interest margin) one must have a very good reason to price a service below its costs.

Of course, at some times and in some markets reasons do exist for pricing below cost. And as we shall see in a few pages, it might be smart for you to price slightly below cost, if certain conditions prevail.

But a beginning point in the pricing of your NOW account, or any other deposit service, should be a complete understanding of your costs and sources of revenue. Once we understand these, we are in a better position to develop our pricing strategies in light of specific marketing, earnings, and growth objectives.

NOW Account Costs

Many have said that from the banker's point of view the NOW account is the worst of both worlds. NOW accounts are like checking accounts in that they have very high operating costs. And they are like time deposits in that they offer the bank a narrower interest margin than checking accounts, since banks are obliged to pay interest on the balance.

TABLE 2.2   NOW Account Activity Costs Compared to
Checking Account Activity Costs

	NOW Account	Checking Account
Cost per debit	$ .12	$ .12
Cost per deposit	.15	.24
Cost per transit item	.06	.07
Account maintenance	3.39	3.24

Source: *Functional Cost Analysis*, Federal Reserve, 1980.

Let's study these costs in greater detail.

NOW account activity costs are virtually the same as checking account activity costs, as can be seen from Table 2.2.

In fact, the slight difference is due to the makeup of the two FCA sub-samples (there were different groups of banks making up the NOW Account sample and the checking account sample). In fact, it is safe to say that for your bank your checking account and NOW account activity costs should be identical. So for the rest of our analysis we'll use the FCA checking costs we've been using throughout this book.

Loaded Activity Costs

The one relevant difference between checking accounts and NOW accounts is the difference in the number of checks written each month. As we remember from our earlier chapter of checking, the average account holder writes sixteen checks per month. The average NOW account holder, on the other hand writes only twelve. This reduces the average total loaded transaction cost, as you can see in Table 2.3.

So, as we can see, NOW accounts carry slightly lower activity and, as a result, are slightly less costly (from strictly an operating cost viewpoint) than checking accounts. But, as we'll see, even though the

NOW accounts are less costly to keep track of from an operating viewpoint, the fact that you pay interest on them makes their total cost to your bank much higher than a checking account. And, as we'll see, you'll want a higher price for your NOW account than your checking account.

As shown in Table 2.3 we must recover $.22 per check, plus the $3.39 account maintenance per month.

TABLE 2.3 Monthly NOW Account Functional Cost Analysis

Function	Cost	Activity	Total Cost
Checks (Debits)	$ .12	12	$1.44
Deposits	.24	2.7	.65
Transit Items	.07	7.5	.53
			$2.62

Fully Loaded Cost Per Check Written = $2.62 ÷ 12 = $.22

Account Maintenance $3.39 per month

Total Monthly Cost = $6.01

Total Yearly Cost = $72.12

Incremental vs. Fully Absorbed Costs

While it's our opinion that all costs are variable in the long run, short run pricing strategies may call for a price to cover incremental costs and contribute something to overhead until the overall shifts in market share settle down. Again, the Functional Cost Studies can be helpful. In the typical middle-sized bank ($50 to $200 million) the ratio of non-officer full time equivalent demand deposit personnel (tellers, bookkeeping, proof) to checking accounts is about 1:270; or, stated differently, for every 270 accounts you lose, you can reduce your demand deposit staff by one. Assuming your typical demand deposit employee earns $12,000 per year, each of the 270 accounts would be burdened with $44.44. This salary is an incremental cost, since if you did not have the accounts, you would not need the employee. The other incremental costs relate primarily to the account maintenance function. If you send monthly statements at a cost of $.35 per statement, this cost per year would be $4.20.

	Incremental Costs Per Year Per Account
Non-Officer Salaries	$44.44
Monthly Statements @ $.35	4.20
Total	$48.64

So, the typical account's cost would be $48.64 incremental cost and $23.48 fixed cost (the fixed cost is the incremental cost deducted from the total yearly cost; allocated costs of building, officer salaries, etc.). Or to simplify future use of this concept, let's just say that about 67% of our transaction costs are incremental. (It should be noted that this is actually a "semi-variable" cost, since 270 accounts must be lost before any savings occurs. For simplicity, we will *treat* it as an incremental cost, since the key point is its "controllable" nature.

NOW Account Activity About Equal to Checking

The average NOW account customer writes only four fewer checks per month than the checking customer. Probably this is due to their demographic characteristics. But for purposes of structuring your NOW account pricing, you should assume that its activity will approximate checking activity, since people tend to view a NOW account as an alternate type of checking account.

Great Variation in Checking Activity

While the functional costs outlined above exhibit very little variation from one bank to the next due to "state of the art" operating methods, there is tremendous variation in consumer check-writing behavior. For example, the Functional Cost Analysis program suggests that the national averages* are:

  12   checks per month

  2.7   deposits

  7.5   transit items

  *$50 to $200 million bank, FCA, Federal Reserve

Studies done by Whittle, Raddon, Motley & Hanks, Inc. reveal that this average may vary from 10 checks to 40 checks depending upon the market served and the pricing structure offered. For example, if a bank were to offer a NOW account with a very low minimum balance in an affluent, younger suburb, its average activity may exceed 40 checks per month. While a rural bank offering "dime-a-time" pricing to an older market may experience average activity of 12 checks per month.

Sample Your NOW Customer Base

The only way for you to correctly price your NOW account is to know your customer's *median* average monthly check writing activity. To get this, you need to contact your data processor; or if they cannot provide you with the figure, you'll have to sample your account base using the procedure described in chapter 3.

After you've finished your sample, you'll want to array the sample by size to find the *median* average (the middle number) since it is the best measure of central tendency in a case like this.

In this case the median is 12, while the mean or arithmetic average is 15.67. And in cases like this where the mean can be influenced by a few large numbers, the median is often a better number.

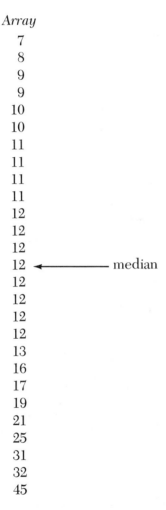

Array

7
8
9
9
10
10
11
11
11
11
12
12
12
12 ←——————— median
12
12
12
12
13
16
17
19
21
25
31
32
45

Average Total Cost

To obtain the average total monthly cost, then, we simply multiply our average (median) activity of 12 checks times our "loaded" activity cost of $.218 per check to obtain our total transaction cost of $2.62. We add our fixed monthly maintenance cost of $3.39 and our total average monthly cost would be $6.01.

> *Average Monthly NOW Costs*
>
> | 12 checks @ $.218 | = | $2.62 |
> |---|---|---|
> | Account Maintenance | = | 3.39 |
> | Total | = | $6.01 |

On an annual basis, this cost would be $72.12.

Incremental Costs

This $72.12 is, of course, the total fully absorbed cost. But we may want to split out the incremental cost from this total for pricing purposes. Given the 67% incremental-to-total cost ratio we developed earlier, we can estimate the two categories on both a monthly and yearly basis.

	Monthly	*Yearly*
Allocated Overhead Cost	$1.98	$23.76
Incremental Cost	4.03	48.36
	$6.01	$72.12

As we have stated, all costs are variable in the long run, and in an industry like ours with earnings insufficiency it is hoped that pricing formulas will reflect total, fully absorbed costs, since significant short-run shifts in transaction account market shares are rare.

Truncation

Some financial institutions used the NOW account introduction as an opportunity to implement check truncation, or to eliminate the practice of returning the actual checks to customers each month. Rather, checks would be microfilmed and destroyed or stored elsewhere.

While I have seen no definitive studies or projected cost savings, it is unlikely that they would be significant in the short run. About

45% of the incremental costs (direct labor) developed earlier are for the salaries on non-teller personnel (i.e., proof operators, bookkeeping, check filing). If the cost of these functions was reduced by as much as 50% the total cost of the transaction account would fall by about 15%, assuming that customers still got some sort of descriptive statement each month. In the example above, the total cost of the NOW would fall from $72.12 a year to $61.30. (67% total direct labor × 45% back room labor × 50% savings.)

Of course, this does not consider the additional costs associated with any special equipment required to operationalize check truncation.

NOTE: This analysis of check truncation is intended as a suggested evaluation rationale. Specific check truncation programs may offer greater or less cost savings.

Operating Costs — In Conclusion

In my opinion, the Functional Cost Analysis program offered by your local Federal Reserve Bank is an excellent management tool available at a reasonable cost.

As we've seen, a NOW account has basically the same costs as a checking account. And as with a checking account, the greatest factor influencing costs is the number of checks people write.

If your bank participates in the Functional Cost Analysis Program, simply use these costs and activity figures. If you do not participate, simply use the average costs provided here and sample your own DDA base to determine likely activity.

The examples in the remainder of this chapter will make use of the following cost and activity assumptions.

	Monthly cost	Yearly cost
12 checks/month @ $2.18 (loaded)	$2.62	$31.44
Account maintenance	$3.39	$40.68
Total costs	$6.01	$72.12
Incremental costs (67%)	$4.03	$48.36

Interest Costs

By law, NOW accounts may not pay more than 5¼% interest. The following analysis will use 5¼% as the interest rate, though you may want to substitute your specific rate should the law change or should you elect to use a different rate or one adjusted for compounding.

The fact that NOW accounts pay interest is what changes their pricing and market dramatically since, as we'll see, this additional, purely variable cost reduces the bank's interest margin and stretches out the breakeven balance so far that we call NOW accounts "checking accounts for high balance customers."

Minimum vs. Average Balance

One issue you'll have to face immediately is whether to pay interest on a customer's average balance during a period or on the low balance. A NOW account is like a checking account in that there is a volatile relationship between a person's average balance and their minimum balance.

Studies of checking accounts reveal the following relationship between minimum and average balances.

Average balance	Minimum balance
$ 50	$ 12
$ 150	$ 40
$ 250	$ 90
$ 350	$160
$ 450	$225
$ 550	$275
$ 750	$425
$1250	$785

Of course NOW accounts will carry typically higher balances. And we estimate that the volatility will be less as the average balances increase. Of course, some people will be attracted to NOW accounts and continue their low balance, high volatility behavior. It is thus estimated that the following relationships might exist for NOW accounts:

Average NOW Balance	*Estimated Minimum Balance*	
$ 50	$ 12	
150	40	
250	90	
350	160	
450	225	
550	275	
750	425	
850	540	
950	593	
1050	656	
1150	718	
1250	785	⎫
2250	1350	⎪
2750	1500	⎬ Likely NOW Account Users
3250	2000	⎪
3750	2500	⎪
4250	3000	⎭

Given this relationship between average balance and minimum balance, it is interesting to see how total NOW interest costs vary by whether you elect to pay interest on the average or on the minimum balance.

TABLE 2.4   NOW Account Interest Costs Per Year:
Average vs. Minimum Balance

Average	Minimum	5¼% Interest on Average	5¼% Interest on Minimum
$ 50	$ 12	$ 2.63	$ .63
150	40	7.88	2.10
250	90	13.13	4.73
350	160	18.38	8.40
450	225	23.63	11.81
550	275	28.88	14.44
750	425	39.38	22.31
1250	785	65.63	41.21
1650	1031	86.63	54.13
2250	1350	118.13	70.88
2750	1500	144.38	78.75
3250	2000	170.63	105.00
3750	2500	196.88	131.25
4250	3000	223.13	157.50
6000	4260	223.13	157.50

Once a person's average balance exceeds $1,000 the volatility
between average and minimum balance moderates, but is still significant. And the difference between paying interest on the average vs.
minimum balance in dollars and cents can be dramatic at these higher
balances. For example, the typical NOW account carries an average
balance of about $6,000. If it can be assumed that this account's
minimum balance is $4,000 there is a significant difference in interest
costs:

5¼% Interest on $4,000 Minimum	5¼% Interest on $6,000 Average
$210	$315

The typical middle-sized bank ($50 to $200 million) has about 2700 such accounts. This $105 annual difference times 2700 accounts can mean a $283,500 net earnings differential! Or stated differently, if this bank paid interest on the minimum, its effective cost of money drops from 5% to 3.5%.

Experience

In New England most banks elected to pay interest on the average balance. And there may be good reason. The early NOW account adopter tended to be financially more sophisticated and, as result, more inclined to take issue with the practice of paying on the minimum.

Moreover, consumers in general are typically happier with maximum rates of interest and compensatory service charges than with slick ways to chisel people out of their interest. Even if the actual net cost is higher, people value simplicity, straightforwardness, and fairness.

As we'll see later, we can set our pricing parameters to recover all costs. And an argument can be made to do it in the way consumers prefer. This may make your pricing appear somewhat higher at first, but when you consider that you pay interest on the total deposit, not the lowest balance during the month, the effect is devastating!

Graphic Presentation of Costs

To further prepare you to set your NOW account pricing, it is helpful to develop a two-dimension representation of the costs. Using data developed above, Exhibit 4 illustrates why a NOW account is different from a checking account. Defining the activity cost ($6.01 per month or $72.12 per year) as a fixed cost which does not vary with the balance level in the account, and the interest cost as a pure variable cost, produces total cost figures well in excess of checking costs. You may, of course, use the $48.36 cost figure if you only wish to consider variable operating costs.

And as we shift our attention from costs to revenues, we must keep in mind that this interest cost continues in direct proportion to the size of the account. This produces a narrow interest margin and as we'll see, a fairly high breakeven balance!

EXHIBIT 4   Annual NOW Account Costs

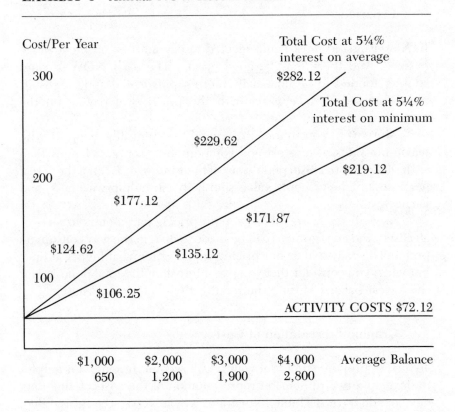

Cost/Per Year

Total Cost at 5¼% interest on average

300     $282.12

Total Cost at 5¼% interest on minimum

$229.62

200     $219.12

$177.12

$171.87

$124.62 $135.12

100

$106.25

ACTIVITY COSTS $72.12

	$1,000	$2,000	$3,000	$4,000	Average Balance
	650	1,200	1,900	2,800	

SOURCES OF REVENUE & BREAKEVEN ANALYSIS

As bankers know, when it comes to covering transaction account costs, there are two potential sources of income: earnings from balances and explicit fees. With checking accounts, where there is clearly a service component to the product, it is a well established idea to charge explicit fees for accounts that provide insufficient balances. But with savings accounts, the concept is fairly new. As has been discussed NOW accounts are perceived as interest-bearing checking accounts. And this suggests that the basic pricing concepts underlying checking accounts should also serve NOW accounts. We must take great care, however, in understanding and measuring the lower net interest margin provided by NOW account deposits.

Net Interest Margin

The net interest margin is the value to the bank of your depositor's money as you invest it in loans and other investments. It is computed by taking your *net-asset yield* and subtracting your *interest costs*. It is analagous to a retail store's gross margin in that with it your bank must pay all salaries, occupancy, overhead, and other expenses plus return a profit to the bank. The net interest margin is the most important source of cost recovery and profit to a bank; and it determines the breakeven level for each of the various sources of funds, including NOW accounts.

A bank's net interest margin and the profitability of its various sources of funds is determined by two variables: the bank's yield on earning assets and its asset mix. Generally, the higher the yield on earning assets, the more profitable your sources of funds and the *lower* the minimum economic deposit size.

Determining Asset Yield

As we move into an environment of deregulation, it is very important for managers of financial institutions to take an "asset and liability" point of view when deciding how to invest their various sources of funds. Generally speaking, interest sensitive deposits (e.g., large CDs and public funds) should be invested in interest-sensitive loans/investments of similar maturity whose yields provide adequate net interest margins. When looking at the very large sources of funds such as $100,000 CDs, this is a fairly straightforward task, and one that most financial managers do intuitively. When we look below this incrementally costly and interest-sensitive source of funds into a bank's core deposits (of which NOW accounts are a part) the question of relevant asset yield becomes a little more elusive. When we think about investing core deposits, it is probable that some of this money will go into each of the following "use of funds" categories (and maybe others):

- Investment portfolio
- Real estate loans
- Installment loans
- Commercial loans

To simplify our analysis, we will make the assumption that each dollar of core deposits will be allocated to the "earning asset portfolio" according to our desired mix of assets. The question then becomes: "What is my average yield on earnings assets?"

The answer is a combination of two things — the yields on your various assets *and* the mix of these assets.

Gross Yield vs. Yield After Operating Costs

Just as FCA studies show us that there are operating costs associated with acquiring deposits, so are there operating costs associated with using funds. In other words, when we make a loan, we incur costs: the salary of the loan officer and credit analyst; the credit application and analysis procedure; developing the loan contract; and the losses on bad loans. These costs must come out of the potential income stream of the loan before the yield after operating costs can be used to determine NOW account and other deposit pricing structures.

FCA Data

In a sample of $50 to $200 million banks, nationwide, the Functional Cost Analysis reveals the following gross yields, operating costs and "yields prior to costs of money" for the years 1973 through 1980.

TABLE 2.5 Functional Cost Analysis

Use of Funds	% Gross Yield	% Operating Costs & Loan Losses (Excluding Costs of Money)	% Yield Prior to Cost of Money
Investments (Taxable Equivalent)			
1973	7.40	.13	7.27
1974	8.21	.14	8.07
1975	7.84	.13	7.71
1976	7.88	.13	7.75
1977	7.87	.14	7.73
1978	8.34	.15	8.19
1979	9.37	.16	9.21
1980	10.56	.16	10.40
1981	12.62	.16	12.46
Real Estate Loans			
1973	7.48	.70	6.78
1974	7.88	.72	7.16
1975	8.07	.77	7.30
1976	8.38	.81	7.57
1977	8.65	.85	7.80
1978	8.85	.81	8.04
1979	9.23	.74	8.49
1980	9.70	.75	8.95
1981	10.41	.78	9.63
Installment Loans			
1973	10.33	3.36	6.97
1974	10.78	3.44	7.34
1975	11.16	3.64	7.52
1976	11.33	3.60	7.73
1977	11.32	3.38	7.94
1978	11.53	3.06	8.47
1979	12.07	2.79	9.28
1980	13.15	2.89	10.26
1981	14.84	3.32	11.52

TABLE 2.5   *(continued)*

Use of Funds	% Gross Yield	% Operating Costs & Loan Losses (Excluding Costs of Money)	% Yield Prior to Cost of Money
Commercial Loans			
1973	7.98	1.30	6.68
1974	9.65	1.39	8.26
1975	9.02	1.58	7.44
1976	8.63	1.70	6.93
1977	8.64	1.65	6.99
1978	9.56	1.67	7.89
1979	11.61	1.38	10.23
1980	13.78	1.54	12.24
1981	16.91	1.62	15.29

It is interesting to note that while the gross yields differ greatly, the yields after operating costs are more comparable. The operating costs associated with various uses of funds differ greatly and serve to nearly equalize the relevant yields.

Asset Mix

The other important determinant of the relevant average asset yield is the *asset mix*. Each bank is unique in this regard and you should use your own bank's data, if possible. The following profile published by the Federal Reserve is based upon the upper quartile of all banks participating in the Functional Cost Analysis. This *Performance Characteristics of High Earning Banks* publication suggests the following asset mix as typical of high earners:

Asset	% of Earning Assets
Investments	38.5%
Real Estate	21.9%
Installments	16.0%
Commercial	23.8%

Weighted Average

Given this asset mix and the prior computations, a weighted average asset yield after operating costs might be similar to the one shown in Table 2.6

TABLE 2.6   Weighted Average Asset Yield

	% Yield After Operating Costs (1980) ×	% of Earning Assets +	Weighted Factor
Investments	10.40	.385	4.00%
Real Estate	8.95	.219	1.96%
Installments	10.26	.160	1.64%
Commercial	12.24	.236	2.89%
Weighted Average			10.49%

In conclusion, if we were to assume that all core deposits were to be used in equal magnitudes to fund the earning asset portfolio, this portfolio would earn (after *asset* operating costs) 10.49%.

NOTE: If your bank has a very high percentage of interest sensitive deposits (i.e., large CDs), you may want to reduce your "pooled asset base" by the specific assets whose earning characteristics most nearly reflect the condition of these CDs. Typically, these assets would be specific commercial loans or investments. After these are removed, use the methodology outlined above to determine your relevant yield on pooled assets.

Future Trend in Asset Yields

We live in a very dynamic and capital-short economy. And it is impossible to be an alert banker today and not realize that asset yield is a variable that will change over time. The central question which we are seeking to answer is "Given relevant yields, what is my minimum economic deposit size on my various core deposit services, such as NOW accounts."

The following tables show that each use of funds has exhibited greater or lesser instability in its yield after operating costs.

TABLE 2.7   Yield After Operating Costs.

Source	Yield After Operating Costs	Secular Trend
Investments		
1973	7.27	Short term fluctuations;
1974	8.07	long term rising
1975	7.71	
1976	7.75	
1977	7.73	
1978	7.79	
1979	9.21	
1980	10.40	
Real Estate		
1973	6.78	
1974	7.16	
1975	7.30	Rising
1976	7.57	
1977	7.80	
1978	7.44	
1979	8.49	
1980	8.95	
Investment		
1973	6.97	
1974	7.34	
1975	7.52	Rising
1976	7.73	
1977	7.94	
1978	7.66	
1979	9.28	
1980	10.26	

TABLE 2.7 *(continued)*

Source	Yield After Operating Costs	Secular Trend
Commercial		
1973	6.68	
1974	8.26	
1975	7.44	Fluctuating and rising
1976	6.93	
1977	6.99	
1978	7.37	
1979	10.23	
1980	12.24	

What we need is a relevant asset yield over the next few years, say two years, to help us determine our minimum economic deposit size for our NOW account. Given these yields and trends, we might make the following calculations.

TABLE 2.8   Expected Yield After Operating Costs on Average Earning Assets

Use of Funds	Secular Character	Expected Net Yield Next 2 Years	% of Earning Assets	Weight Factor
Investments	Fluctuating and rising secular trend	11.00%	38.5%	4.24
Real Estate	Rising	9.5%	21.9%	2.08
Installment	Rising	11.00%	16.0%	1.76
Commercial	Volatile — but	12.00%	23.6%	2.83
	Weighted average future yield after operating cost on earning assets			10.91

Note: This example assumes that the future assets mix will be the same. Interestingly, installment loans enjoy the second highest yield while commanding the fewest dollars. In developing your bank's relevant future asset yield, you may wish to change your asset mix to reflect such profit improvement potential.

Float and Reserves

Of course, not every dollar of your NOW account can be invested directly into the earning assets. Some of it is always in the process of collection (float) and some is held in required reserves. Functional cost studies suggest that about 91.5% of the NOW account average balance actually will be earning money.

To adjust for this uninvested money, simply reduce your anticipated spread accordingly.

$$\text{Anticipated Spread} \times \% \text{ Invested} = \text{Value of NOW Deposits}$$
$$(10.91\%\text{--}5.25\%) \times .915 = 5.18\%$$

Management Factor

Based upon the above calculations, you might expect your NOW deposits to be worth 5.18% over the next two years, a reasonable pricing horizon. But because of local conditions, management changes, or other conditions, you may want to adjust this subjectively. Pricing is as much an art as a science, and intangibles must be considered.

Breakeven NOW Balance

We have now developed all of the cost and revenue information required to compute our breakeven NOW average balance. Depending, of course, on which costs you feel are relevant, there will be different breakeven points.

To compute the breakeven average balance, simply divide the annual operating costs by the net interest margin, since these activity costs must be recovered by investing a person's NOW balances in your various earning assets.

$$\text{Breakeven Balance} = \frac{\text{Annual Operating Costs}}{\text{Net Asset Yield} - \text{Interest Cost}}$$

Full Cost Breakeven

If you want to recover your NOW account's fully absorbed cost:

$$\frac{\text{Full Cost}}{\text{Interest Margin}} = \frac{\$72.12}{5.18\%} = \$1,392 \text{ average balance}$$

Incremental Cost Breakeven

If you feel you're likely to face still more local price competition, you may elect to recover just your incremental operating costs, which as we've said are about 67% of fully absorbed costs.

$$\frac{\text{Incremental Cost}}{\text{Interest Margin}} = \frac{\$48.64}{5.18\%} = \$934 \text{ average balance}$$

These breakeven points are significantly higher than comparable checking account breakeven points; and it is for this reason that banks should consider positioning NOW accounts as "checking accounts for high balance customers."

Service Fees

Keeping this positioning concept in mind, the service charge, then, is designed to recover any operating cost not recovered by the average balance. Or stated more simply, whenever anyone's balance falls below breakeven, his or her account should be charged.

Minimum vs. Average

Because they appear lower and are easier to understand, many banks elect to use minimum balances rather than averages on published fee schedules. For example, the following two NOW account prices are the same:

#1
Minimum NOW Balance

During Month	Monthly Fee
+ $1,200	No Charge
$0 to $1,200	$6.00

#2
Average NOW Balance

During Month	Monthly Fee
+ $2,000	No Charge
$0 to $2,000	$6.00

Yet, consumers will invariably think #2 is more costly.

To protect your financially sophisticated NOW customer whose average balance may exceed $2,000, but whose minimum may fall below $1,000, simply program your computer to waive all service charges if the customer's average balance is adequate. Such a silent parameter need not appear on any published document. It is there to protect your higher balance accounts.

Flat Fee vs. Per Item Charge

Depending upon how you price your checking account, you may elect to price on a flat monthly fee basis or on a per item basis, if your NOW customer's minimum falls below your breakeven point.

Generally, it's a good idea to price your NOW account and checking account using a similar structure (i.e., flat fee or per item fee), since this promotes ease of understanding at the new accounts desk.

There are, of course, advantages and disadvantages to both methods. Consumers often prefer the flat fee method (e.g., $6.00 if your balance falls below $1,000) because it is simple and easy to understand. They are more concerned with checkbook accuracy than the few cents a month difference.

On the other hand, per item charges tend to discourage check writing and control operating costs.

Many bankers combine the two with a flat fee for basic activity (e.g., 20 checks) and impose an excess usage fee (e.g., $4.15 per item) when actual activity exceeds this.

Alternate Pricing Structures

The monthly fee, however it is charged, is designed to be the slack variable in the pricing equation. When a customer's balance falls below breakeven, the fee covers your costs.

Given the sample data we've devloped thus far, the fee required to breakeven at various NOW balances would look like that in Table 2.9 for our *four basic cost structures.*

TABLE 2.9   Fully Absorbed Costs/Interest on Average Balance

NOW Balance Average	Minimum	Fully Absorbed Operating Costs	Interest Margin 5.18%	Annual Profit (Loss)	Monthly Service Charge to Breakeven
$ 50	$ 12	$72.12	$ 2.59	($69.53)	$5.79
$ 150	$ 40	$72.12	$ 7.77	($64.35)	$5.36
$ 250	$ 90	$72.12	$ 12.95	($59.17)	$4.93
$ 350	$ 160	$72.12	$ 18.13	($53.99)	$4.50
$ 450	$ 225	$72.12	$ 23.31	($48.81)	$4.07
$ 550	$ 275	$72.12	$ 28.49	($43.63)	$3.64
$ 750	$ 425	$72.12	$ 38.85	($33.27)	$2.77
$1,250	$ 785	$72.12	$ 64.75	($ 7.37)	$ .61
$2,250	$1,350	$72.12	$116.55	$44.43	$0
$2,750	$1,500	$72.12	$142.45	$70.33	$0
$3,250	$2,000	$72.12	$168.35	$96.23	$0

Smoothing out the rough edges and adding a little profit, this data would translate into these pricing schedules:

Minimum* Monthly NOW Balance	Monthly Fee
+ $1,500 + $1,000	No Charge
$500–$999	$2.00
$0–$499	$6.00

*If your prefer average balances, simply substitute the appropriate average balance.

Another pricing structure might look like this:

Minimum Monthly Balance	Monthly Fee
+ $1,000	No Charge
$0–$999	$6.00

Or, if you prefer the per item formula:

Minimum Monthly Balance	Monthly Fee
+ $1,000	No Charge
$0–$999	$.25 per draft plus $3.00 account maintenance

The structure you choose depends upon your market, but keep it simple and use the same structure you use for checking.

If you elect to cover only incremental operating costs because of anticipated competitive pressure, your monthly fees would look like this:

TABLE 2.10 Incremental Operating Costs/Interest on Average Balance

NOW Balance Average	Minimum	Incremental Operating Costs	Interest Margin 5.18%	Annual Profit (Loss)	Monthly Service Charge to Breakeven
$ 50	$ 12	$48.36	$ 2.59	($45.77)	$3.81
$ 150	$ 40	$48.36	$ 7.77	($40.59)	$3.38
$ 250	$ 90	$48.36	$12.95	($35.41)	$2.95
$ 350	$ 160	$48.36	$18.13	($30.26)	$2.52
$ 450	$ 225	$48.36	$23.31	($25.05)	$2.09
$ 550	$ 275	$48.36	$28.49	($19.89)	$1.66
$ 750	$ 425	$48.36	$38.85	($ 9.88)	$ .82
$1,250	$ 785	$48.36	$64.75	$16.39	$0
$1,650	$1,031	$48.36	$85.47	$37.11	$0

Given this data and these costs, the variable minimum balance NOW account would look like this:

Minimum NOW Balance	Monthly Fee
+ $500	No Charge
$250–$499	$2.00
$0–$249	$4.00

Of course, these fees are approximates. The same range of minimums might also ask for $4.00, $1.00, no charge or $5.00, $3.00, no charge. The idea is that you can leave the all-important balance ranges intact while changing the related fees. And it is the feature of flexibility that makes this variable minimum balance plan so useful.

A single minimum balance structure would look like this:

Minimum NOW Balance	Monthly Fee
+ $500	No Charge
$0–$499	$4.00

If you use the single minimum balance structure, make your fee a little higher since you are treating the entire group similarly and there are likely to be more accounts toward the lower end if the price is not discouraging.

If you choose the per item approach the structure would look like this:

Minimum NOW Balance	Monthly Fee
+ $500	No Charge
$0–$499	$.20 per draft plus $2.00 account maintenance per month.

Other Structures and Product Line Pricing

These, then, are the basic cost assumptions translated into pricing structures and specific prices. The pricing structures fall into three basic categories:

1. Variable minimum monthly balance
2. Single minimum monthly balance
3. Formula with minimum

I feel that these are the principle pricing structures best suited for the NOW account. The NOW account, by definition, is a product targeted for higher balance customers, since lower balance customers benefit very little as a result of the interest. For example, a person who maintains an average balance of $100.00 would earn $.44 per month (5.25% × 100 ÷ 12).

And if, as recommended, your monthly service charge on such a balance is at least $1.00 higher with your NOW than your checking, your customer is better off with checking.

| Balance | | Checking | Monthly | NOW Earnings | Net |
Average	Minimum	Monthly Fee	Fee	(5.25%)	Cost
$100	$26	$5.00	$6.00	$.44	$5.56

You see, this interest benefits your low balance customer very little, but can cost you greatly. For example, if you priced your NOW and checking exactly the same, people would be encouraged into the NOW. And while the $.44 per month may not be worth that much to your customer, with 10,000 accounts the cost to you could be $52,500 in additional interest costs.

The concept you must follow is *market segmentation*. Give the NOW account to those higher balance customers who'll really benefit from it; and whose balances you don't want to lose. But price it so the lower balance customer gets a better deal with regular checking. This "product line pricing" concept further suggests that the basic pricing structures should be similar.

| Checking | | NOW | |
Minimum Checking Balance	Monthly Fee	Minimum NOW Balance	Monthly Fee
+ 400	No Charge	+ $1,000	No Charge
$0–$399	$5.00	$0–$999	$6.00

Such a pricing concept lets you segment your market and enables you to build a tool for your deposit counselor to explain whether a person is better off in a checking or NOW account.

There are, of course, other basic structures, such as the "club plan" which charges people a flat fee per month regardless of the monthly balance (e.g. $4.00 per month). These clubs often promote unlimited check writing, free use of other services, and insurance, all of which lower the bank's profit margin. These programs have been quite successful in many markets, but generally appeal to the lower balance segments of the market; and, as a result, often encourage significantly higher check writing and operating costs. (Studies consistently show that the check writing behavior of club account holders is nearly double that of regular checking customers.) These characteristics suggest that while club plans might be effective alternatives to NOW accounts for lower balance customers, they would not be good vehicles for the NOW account itself. Your NOW account should be aimed at a fairly small segment of the market; and this may be incompatible with the mass promotion concept underlying flat fee pricing. Moreover, such a plan might encourage the higher balance customers into competitive plans where balances earn customers no service charges.

Of course, it is possible that you could combine the club concept with the minimum balance feature. And from your customer's view this would be fine. This would, however, necessitate that all additional club costs for customers meeting the balance requirements (e.g., insurance) be covered directly from your earnings. Consequently, to effectively price such a plan, you'd have to add these costs to those described above and set appropriately higher minimums. For example, if you took a NOW account priced on a full absorption basis (e.g., $1,000 minimum or $6.00) and added the cost of club benefits, the total cost would be:

	Monthly Cost	Yearly Cost
12 checks @ $.22	$2.64	$31.68
Account Maintenance	$3.39	$40.68
Club benefits	$1.00	$12.00
Total	$7.03	$84.36

Assuming you pay interest on the average balance, your break-even deposit size would be:

$$\frac{\$84.36}{5.18\%} = \$1,628 \text{ average balance}$$

This compares with a non-club breakeven balance of $1,392 and would probably necessitate a pricing structure requiring a minimum of $250 to $500 more per month and a higher conditional fee ($7.00). So the final pricing structure might be $1,500/$7.00 rather than $1,000/$6.00. People in your market might see perceived value in the club equal to this; and they might not.

The same or even stronger criticism can be offered against non-club flat fee or formula arrangements which give no recognition of acceptable balances, since in this method there is no additional perceived value. Such a plan would be very vulnerable to minimum (or average) balance competitive plans, especially among your higher balance customers.

Excess Usage Fees

While consumers dislike them, bankers have a fondness for formula (per item) pricing structures. Bankers feel that they're more equitable or that they relate more closely to their costs. And these opinions are probably true. Nevertheless, consumers don't like them; and in most cases would rather pay $5.00 than $4.24, if the latter number changed each month. People like, and will pay for, convenience and simplicity.

On the other hand, though, flat fees (even with minimum balance plans) encourage more check writing. This is, after all, why people buy checking accounts. But this excess check writing is often confined to a minority of accounts. For example, you might find that your average activity is 15 checks per month, but that 20% of your customers write more than 15 checks. In fact, some of these might write 40, 50, or even 100 checks! And these people should pay extra.

A good way to accomplish this objective is simply to have your basic pricing structure buy a certain number of checks. For example, maybe the $6.00 buys 20 checks. This gives your average customers a little cushion. But you charge $.20 for each excess check.

In this way, you maximize profit on those who write more and those who write less than the average!

Pricing Strategies

Now that we've examined the basic pricing structures, it's time to shift our focus to pricing strategies. By strategy we mean consideration of competitor's likely pricing approaches along side your objectives. For example, if you think your local competitors (be sure to include thrifts) are going to offer free NOW accounts to gain market share, you might want one pricing structure. On the other hand if you suspect that your local competition will price the NOW high to discourage use, you might want a different structure and price level.

Two basic and interrelated factors must be considered when you are developing your pricing strategy: 1) your bank's earnings and growth objective; and 2) the anticipated pricing strategies of your competitors, which generally grows out of *their* growth and earning objectives.

Your Bank's Objectives

Banks today are increasingly bottom line oriented. This is, to a large degree, a recognition of our industry's current earnings squeeze. It also speaks well of the current group of bank CEOs who understand that in an industry as highly leveraged as banking (5% to 8% capital to asset ratios) even future growth objectives depend upon adequate short term earnings. For these and other reasons most high earning bankers would arrange corporate objectives so that growth is consistent with earnings rather than vice versa.

Nevertheless, some financial institutions still favor growth objectives over earnings. In some cases this stems from an honest belief that long run profit maximization might be obtained by pricing below cost in the short run. In other cases growth objectives assume preeminence because of their greater visibility — customers always want higher rates on deposits, lower rates on loans, and free checking — and management's soft heartedness.

Having said this and affirming the opinion that earnings should receive higher priority, I recognize that cases may exist where the disparity between pure earnings vs. pure growth strategies may be less.

For example, if your bank's capital to asset ratio is 5% and declining and your return on average assets is .2%, you probably have no business pricing your NOW account below incremental costs. On the other hand, if your capital is adequate and growing and your return on assets is 2.0%, than you might want to build market share a little, especially if your competitors are poorer earners.

The point is, simply, pricing cannot be done in a vacuum. Pricing is a tool within your competitive marketing mix (along with the product, how you promote it; and your distribution outlet convenience). You must engineer your pricing effort to serve both financial and marketing objectives, given *local* conditions.

The NOW Account Strategy Wheel (Exhibit 5) might help you do this. It starts with the two basic objectives — growth vs. earnings — which your bank might favor in the short run and works toward specific marketing strategies, pricing strategies, and specific prices. You start from the center of this diagram and work outward.

So, first you must decide if your situation calls for a short run growth or an earnings set of objectives.

Generally speaking, the following characteristics relate to banks who *should be* pursuing growth and earnings objectives.

Growth	*Earnings*
• Good earnings	• High growth market
• Stable, non-growth market	• Poorer earnings history
• Strong capital and retained earnings	• Insufficient capital

Of course, these are generalities and you must make your own assessment. This is where management ceases being a science and takes on the character of an art. Making these strategic decisions is difficult because it involves judgment about so many variables.

EXHIBIT 5   NOW Account Strategy Wheel

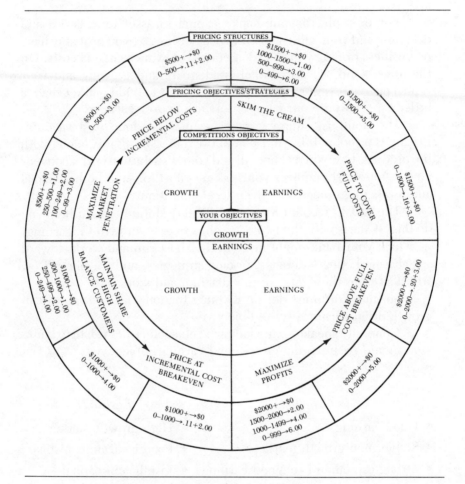

Note: Start in center and work outward.
Assumes interest paid on average balance, all balances are minimums.
© Copyright 1980 Whittle, Raddon, Motley & Hanks, Chicago.

Competitor Objectives and Strategy

Gauging your competitor's strategies is difficult and requires your careful judgment. If you assume a competitor is going to price the

NOW high (e.g., $2,000 minimum) and it actually offers the product free, you could be hurt with the middle market customer — those people keeping less than full cost breakeven but more than incremental cost breakeven. On the other hand, if you knew your competitor was going to offer it free, you could price it to cover incremental costs and keep the middle market customer. But you still might elect not to do this if your earnings were bad.

Simply stated, your pricing strategy involves many variables which must be considered simultaneously. The Strategy Wheel should help in this regard.

Other Elements of Your Market Mix

Although it would be too confusing to try to put them into the Strategy Wheel you must also consider other elements of your NOW account marketing mix. For example, if you have more branches that are better located than your competitor's you have a significant distribution advantage. This should enable you to charge a higher price than you otherwise might.

Also, if your NOW product is differentiated and presumably better structured than your competitor's, you might charge a higher price.

How could your product be different? Let's say that in addition to lowering a customer's fee for NOW balances, you also give credit for savings balances.

This would enable a customer to use his NOW account actively without regard to balance level and keep all of the compensatory balances in a savings account or certificate of deposit that pays perhaps an even higher rate. As long as the balance requirements are properly set, you should not really care. But from the customer's viewpoint, "checking is checking" and "savings is savings." They want interest on both, but may want to keep the two pools of funds separate.

Such a "discount for savings" might enable you to charge a slightly higher price and attract more balance-rich customers.

The kind of "relationship pricing" suggested by this example is not only good from a pricing point of view, it is crucial in the kind of environment many see following the elimination of Regulation Q. In this environment, there will be no built-in incentive for people to split relationships between banks and thrifts (they'll all be able to pay the same interest rates), so banks must create their own economic incentives to encourage customers to bring them their entire deposit relationship.

By this time you should have a pretty good idea of how to price your NOW account. So, let's turn our attention to NOW account implementation, training, and promotion.

IMPLEMENTING NEW NOW ACCOUNT PRICES

By now you should have a fairly good grasp of how you are going to price and position your NOW account in your market. But you might still be wondering about some of the specifics, such as how to introduce a new price, how your promotion might differ if you want to maximize market penetration rather than protect earnings, what letters to send out, or how to train your new accounts people.

Implementation specifics, such as the actual advertising or the wording of introductory letters, are very personal. One person may like a graphic concept; one might prefer something different. And every trainer has his or her own style.

So, unlike the quantitative analysis that preceded this section, the following material is offered as a set of guidelines. You'll want to read the material and the various examples and illustrations, simply to get an idea of what you want to do. Then bring in your various specialists to develop your specifics.

You'll have to consider the following areas of implementation specifics:

1. Product differentiation, if any
2. Training
3. Promotion and advertising

These may all vary depending upon your pricing strategy. For example, if you elect to price the NOW account relatively low to maximize market share, you'll likely have a different promotion and training program than if you were to price it very high and limit its market.

We'll see how the three basic strategies influence these considerations later.

1. Maximize profits, when both you and your competition are earnings oriented
2. Maintain share of high balance market, when you are earnings oriented and your competition is growth oriented
3. Maximize market penetration, when all competitors are growth oriented
4. Increase market share when you are growth oriented and your competitors are earnings oriented.

For now, let's explore each factor.

Product Differentiation

To protect your high balance customers in the face of more favorably priced competitive NOW accounts or to attract more business to your bank, you might want to differentiate your NOW account from your competitor's. In other words, since your price is higher, or since your bank is less convenient, you might need a non-price product feature which makes your NOW account preferable to cheaper or more convenient accounts.

A good way to do this is to offer customers a discount if they maintain other accounts with you. In other words, you let your customer keep his or her compensatory balance in either the NOW account or a separate savings account (which may even pay a little higher interest). Consumers like this flexibility, since many do not want to combine "savings dollars" with "spending dollars." Although bankers draw little distinction between NOWs and savings, consumers do. Blending both balances to them is too dangerous — spending is spending and savings are savings.

Since most people are accustomed to keeping lower checking balances, this feature can be very attractive. And it enables you to offer a product that is demonstrably better than the competitor's product.

Assuming that the compensatory savings deposit generates roughly the same spread, earnings on the first $673 in the savings account covers the annual operating costs ($30.22 — figure from the Functional Cost Analysis) of the savings. The remainder can be used to give credit against NOW activity fees. Given this, you can offer a "free" NOW account to any customer who keeps about $2,000 in a separate regular savings account.

If you extend this savings discount to regular checking customers, whose balances are insufficient for NOW account but who have good savings balances that they want separate from their transaction balances, you can advertise the fact that whether they choose regular checking or NOW checking, the deal can be better'than just interest on checking and hence better than your competitor's product line!

Training

Experience shows that the group of people in your market most sensitive to changes in prices are often your own employees. Some of the bank's customers may feel that banks are part of the government and should not charge for services. This attitude reflects also the consumer view that banking is a facilitative industry. Checking-type accounts are very important to people, yet they take them for granted. A checking account in itself is not important; it's value is that it facilitates the acquisition of products or services. In this way, checking/NOW accounts are like gasoline. Gasoline is important, but the value relates to the car and the transportation.

Also, consumers do not understand banking. They have no appreciation for how insignificant the interest margin really is in dollars and cents. The consumer's view is that "the banks are using all my checking money to get rich, and I'm *entitled* to interest."

Although consumers feel entitled to interest, they do not appreciate that its payment necessitates significantly higher balances, or offsetting fee charges, to recover the operating costs associated with NOW accounts.

The objective of employee training is to educate your customers, *through your employees,* so they know that your pricing rationale is fair, equitable, and realistic.

To achieve this objective, keep the following training guidelines in mind.

1. *Share your analysis with them.*

   After you've "crunched your numbers" and developed your pricing strategy, schedule a meeting or series of meetings and let your employees in on the decision. Encourage questions. Get your CEO or senior management involved, so employees feel that they are part of the team.

   If you are very careful, open, and honest with your employees, they'll support you.

2. *Product Knowledge/Sales Training*

   After your general meeting, break down your new accounts, customer service, and tellers into peer groups for more intensive training.

   Give them samples of the various charts, brochures, and other literature you've devised to explain which customers will benefit from NOWs and which will not.

   Explain to them how they should go about using this information. Then encourage their participation and practice. Nothing engenders support and commitment more than involvement.

If you expect to lose some accounts, admit it in these sessions. Employees feel bad when customers complain and close their accounts. Tell them that with your pricing you expect to lose some customers, but that their job is to explain your program and to keep this figure to a minimum.

When employees want to know how the competition can charge less, explain that their decision may have been made without the knowledge of costs. Or that they chose to price below costs. Explain further that you elected to charge a more rational price in order to continue to hire, train, and compensate good people. Make your employees feel that they are on the winning team in the game that counts — making money to pay salaries.

Promotion

The extent to which — and how — you promote your NOW account will, of course, depend on your pricing strategy. If you charge a high price and want limited usage, you'll want to follow one set of guidelines. While if you choose a low price and want wide usage, you'll follow a different set. Specific guidelines will be covered later in this book.

Checking Accounts For High Balance Customers

For now, let's take a look at some generalities. Many banks will undoubtedly choose to charge a high price for the NOW account, perhaps higher than the competition. These banks may want to limit the product's use to those customers who will be profitable, or at least cover costs.

While the pricing structures discussed earlier can help in this segmentation effort, your promotional materials should be clean, rich looking, and support this idea. Financial services are intangibles; and by virtue of their specialized nomenclature (interest rates, percentages, yields) they are difficult to understand. People appreciate and pay for simplicity.

To help you explain your new NOW account, you'll need a simple, clear-cut brochure. This brochure should explain *what* the NOW account is, how it works, and how it differs from checking. Without getting into specific prices (which may change), you may want to explain that NOW accounts are not for everyone and some people may be dollars and cents ahead with a regular checking account.

The graphics of this brochure should also be clear and simple. People, especially the higher balance customers, do not appreciate "cute" advertising in the financial services industry as much as they might in other industries.

3

Savings Accounts and Certificates of Deposit

For years, the business of banking was fairly straightforward and simple. It involved taking in the fairly abundant low-cost deposits and investing them in loans and other investments at yields sufficient to generate the margins required to cover all operating costs and return a profit. To a large degree these comfortable margins were established by regulatory fiat rather than market forces. Fundamentally, the business of banking is the same. However, the sources of funds are no longer abundant; nor are they cheap. In earlier days, bankers did not concern themselves too greatly with the explicit operating costs of the various sources of funds. These funds generally came in fairly large chunks from commercial businesses or in the form of regular savings deposits whose interest rate was artificially low.

In the past ten to twenty years, however, economic forces have changed the nature of banking. Sources of funds have become less plentiful and more costly. Before moving to this issue of pricing savings and time deposits, it is helpful to put this issue in an historic perspective.

Since the early 1960s our country's principal economic policies have been designed to stimulate the private sector. Government spending and borrowing has generated strong "demand pull" inflationary pressure and, generally speaking, the private sector has responded with a desire for increased growth to accommodate this increase in demand. These forces resulted in a generalized desire in both the private and public sectors for more capital. Business managers began leaving less money in idle demand deposits. As their desire for money grew, they began to cut the middlemen bankers out of the intermediation equation, and the commercial paper market was created.

This overall increase in the demand for funds brought into question the continued viability of Regulation Q, which was adopted to protect banks from the vagaries of the market. During each inflationary period over the past decade, some assault was made on Regulation Q. The effect, over the years, was to increase the overall costs of banking by increasing the costs bankers must pay for their funds.

During each inflationary period, consumers get a little smarter, and as a result, demand a little more return on their dollar. To see this effect, it is helpful to examine the most recent inflationary period.

THE MONEY MARKET CERTIFICATE

As established earlier, a bank makes money by managing the "spread" between its overall cost of funds and the loan/investment yields these funds produce. (This is not to minimize the importance of non-interest expense control and non-interest revenue, but the interest margin does produce the initial profit margin.) And while we will see later in this chapter that we will have to take a segmented pricing view of our various sources of funds, it is interesting to see how inflationary forces affect our overall cost of funds.

A bank's average cost of funds (and thereby its net interest margin), excluding cost of capital, is significantly influenced by its deposit mix. Generally speaking, the more low-cost deposits a bank has, the more attractive its interest margin can be (or the more competitive it can be in establishing loan rates). Prior to 1978 and the Money Market certificate, the typical deposit mix and average cost of funds profile might have looked like the one shown in the appended table.

TABLE 3.1   Deposit Mix and Average Cost of Funds Profile Prior to 1978.

Source	Compounded** Interest Costs	% of Total	Weighted Cost Factor
Demand Deposits	0.00%	25	.00
Regular Savings	5.13%	15	.76
90-Day	5.73%	4	.23
1 Year C/D	6.27%	37	2.32
2½ Year C/D	6.81%	5	.34
4 Year C/D	7.62%	6	.45
6 Year C/D	7.90%	4	.32
8 Year C/D	8.17%	4	.33
		100	4.75%

** Daily Compounding

It is necessary to see the overall importance of deposit mix in determining a bank's cost of funds. In this example, the bank's cost — 4.75% — is less than any particular source of savings/time deposits. This is because 25% of the bank's funds come in the form of demand deposits. This does not mean these funds are "free." The costs are simply non-interest costs. And, as we've seen, the key is to recover these costs through balances or explicit fees.

Now, let's look at the same bank's cost of funds profile in 1982.

TABLE 3.2   Current Cost of Funds Profile

Source	Interest Cost	% of Total	Cost Factor Weighted
Demand Deposits	0.00%	20%	.00%
NOW Accounts	5.25%	10%	.53%
Regular Savings	5.25%	10%	.53%
6 Month MMCD	11.00%	40%	4.40%
2½ Year MMCD	12.00%	10%	1.20%
All Other Regulation Q Deposits	6.50%	10%	.65%
Weighted Average			7.31%

During the four year period from 1978 to 1982, this bank's average cost of funds increased from 4.75% to 7.31%. This represents an increase in excess of 54%.

This is a fairly typical example of the principle articulated earlier — during each period of inflation, consumers learn a little more, expect a little more, and a bank's cost of funds increases. So great are the current inflationary pressures that an extrapolation of this trend will result in banks paying nearly money market rates on *all* sources of deposits.

While such a trend is applauded by enlightened bankers who desire to compete in a more unrestricted way, it will, nevertheless, result in some fundamental changes in deposit pricing and marketing. The practice of packaging free operating services (i.e., accepting deposits, making withdrawals, providing insurance, sending information) into a savings product paying sub-market interest rates will begin to erode. As consumers demand market rates of return on all deposits, bankers will have little alternative than to charge explicit fees for service (or pay lower rates of interest on uneconomic deposit levels).

As we'll see later in this chapter, as deposit rates of interest go up, the minimum deposit amount required to recover the activity costs of savings accounts increases. This economic fact directly conflicts with the current political and regulatory desire to pay higher rates of interest on smaller deposits. As deposit sizes fall, the activity cost component increases in its relative significance. And this makes the notion more viable that the costs of such service should be recovered with a fee.

The practice of charging a fee for savings account activity is relatively new. And it may take a while for consumers to accept it. Nevertheless, it is the direction in which we are moving. In the interim, however, there are other pricing options that we will explore in this chapter.

Other pricing options to be considered are:

- Not paying interest on uneconomic deposit levels — a defensive strategy
- Encouraging higher deposit levels through incentives — an offensive strategy
- Focusing marketing attention on segments that typically maintain higher balance levels thus avoiding the problem

We'll end this chapter by exploring a number of specifics relative to each of these strategies. But one should keep in mind the ultimate posture of charging explicit fees for services and paying market rates for deposits. You should begin to explore the feasibility of charging fees on low balance savings accounts.

A Word of Caution

As we've seen, checking accounts are convenience dominated services exhibiting relatively little price elasticity. Savings accounts are influenced but not dominated by convenience factors; moreover, they are available from thrifts as well as banks. Pricing strategies designed to relate savings balances and/or fees to costs are, as a result, much more likely to encourage people to move such accounts. If the cost/revenue/breakeven analysis is done carefully, however, this fact should not greatly disturb bank managers. Given the commentary at the beginning of this book, the most important strategy for a bank to follow is one that assures profitable growth. As we'll see, the problem of the low balance savings account is nearly as great as that of the low balance checking account. FCA studies reveal that 41% of all regular savings accounts are under $100.

Recognizing that the elimination of low balance savings accounts carries the same opportunity to "export" loss accounts that exists with checking accounts, let us turn our attention to the question of the costs of various time sources of deposits and their related minimum economic deposit levels.

SAVINGS AND TIME ACCOUNT COSTS

The various savings/time account products have two cost components which must be considered in developing the breakeven balance/fee trade off. Each product has an operating cost component which reflects the costs of the various activities performed on the various products (i.e., opening the account, closing the acount, accepting deposits, making withdrawals, paying interest, and maintaining the account on the computer). These costs, while lower than the activity costs associated with a checking account, are influential in determining the minimum economic deposit required in the account before all costs are covered.

Savings/time products also carry another cost — the interest paid on the deposit. This cost is purely variable and relates strictly to the size of the deposit. Economically, as we shall see, its effect is to reduce the "earnings credit" value of the deposit to the bank. In other words, if we can invest savings deposits in our loan/investment portfolio and earn 10.52% (after deducting loan/investment operating costs), but must pay depositors 5.39% (5.39% is the effective cost of compounding 5.25%), then our "spread" or net interest margin on such deposits is only 5.13%.

It is with this 5.13% (or whatever, for various savings products) that we must first recover our activity costs; and then begin to return a profit to the bank.

Activity Costs

FCA studies suggest the following activity costs for various regular savings product functions.

TABLE 3.3   Activity Costs for Savings Product Functions.

Function	Cost Per Function	Annual Activity	Total Annual Cost
Deposits	$ .56	5.12	$ 2.87
Withdrawals	$ 1.09	3.93	$ 4.27
Account Maintenance	$14.14	1.00	$14.14
Interest Postings	$ 1.98	4.00	$ 7.93
Open Account*	$ .62*	N/A	$ .62
Close Account*	$ .37*	N/A	$ .37
			$30.20

*These figures are the actual functional costs divided by five. This was done to spread these one-time costs over the average five-year life of a savings account. To obtain the actual functional cost multiply by five.

The annualized operating cost of a regular savings account is $30.20.

Annualized Costs

It is important to express operating costs on an "annualized basis" since, as we'll see, they are recovered with a net interest margin expressed on an annual basis.

CERTIFICATES OF DEPOSIT

Another source of funds for banks is the certificate of deposit. These accounts afford customers the opportunity to earn different amounts of interest for varying lengths of time. Since immediate liquidity is not a feature of a certificate of deposit, its operating costs are usually lower than either checking accounts or savings accounts.

FCA studies reveal the following activity costs of certificates:

Function	Cost
Open account	$1.89
Close account	$1.47
Pay interest	$1.54
Account maintenance	$3.36 (annually)

To develop the needed annualized costs, one must develop the total cost of each CD to maturity and then divide by that maturity.

One Year CD	Annualized Cost
Open account	$ 1.89
Close account	$ 1.47
Pay interest (4 times)	$ 6.16
Account maintenance	$ 3.36
	$12.88 ÷ 1 = $12.88

2½ Year CD	
Open account	$ 1.89
Close account	$ 1.47
Pay interest (10 months)	$15.40
Account maintenance	$ 8.40
	$27.16 ÷ 2.5 = $10.86

Using similar computations, we can develop the following schedule of annualized operating costs and interest cost of the various sources of funds. (Annualized money market costs assume two CDs per year [i.e., money "rolls over"] with interest paid after each 6 month maturity.)

TABLE 3.4   Annualized Operating Costs

Source of Funds	Annualized Operating Costs
Regular Savings	$30.20
90-Day MMCD*	$22.96
6 Month MMCD*	$13.16
1 Year CD	$12.88
2½ Year CD	$10.86

*Annualized money market costs assume two or four CDs per year (i.e., money "rolls over") with interest paid after each maturity.

Breakeven Analysis

Bankers today are generally faced with two types of savings accounts: regular savings accounts, where the interest rates are established by Regulation Q maximums, and those where the interest rate is not specified or floats with some market rate.

The breakeven equation can be used to help set pricing parameters for both types of accounts. In the case of the regular savings account, you are solving for the minimum balance, since regulations establish the interest rate. To obtain the breakeven minimum balance, one simply divides the annualized operating costs ($30.20) by the associated net interest margin (10.52% − 5.39%). (5.39% is the effective cost after compounding of a 5¼% account). The result is $588, the breakeven balance for a regular savings account. Below this level, the account is unprofitable, while above this level the account is earning money for the bank.

In the case of a money market certificate, the minimum balance levels themselves are set by regulations. Also, the regulations establish ceiling rates of interest above which the bank cannot pay. In this case, the breakeven equation is used to compute the spread the bank must obtain on the deposit to cover the annualized operating costs.

$$\frac{\text{Breakeven}}{\text{Spread}} = \frac{\text{Annualized Operating Costs}}{\text{Required Balance Minimum}}$$

In the case of a six month money market certificate, the annualized operating costs are $13.16; and the required minimum balance is $2,500. This produces a breakeven spread of .52%. In other words, the banker must be able to lay off the deposit in an asset whose yield is .52% above what the market says he can pay for the deposit.

Of course, this .52% spread is just a breakeven spread. Since most banks are not in business to breakeven, it is appropriate that some profit should be added in. As we'll see shortly, this should be in the neighborhood of 1% to 2%. So the actual required spread on six month money market certificates should be between 1.13% and 2.13%.

The key thing to remember in pricing money market certificates is that the job really has been done for you already. The government has already set the price and your only decision is whether to participate. To guide you in making this decision, you should try to maintain an appropriate spread of 125 to 225 basis points on assets of similar maturity.

Short Term Money Market CD Losses

This expectation raises a key question. Where did these deposits come from and where will they go when rates start falling? The first question is fairly easy to answer. Most of the funds come from the *existing* core deposit bases of banks offering the product. (Interestingly, banks that did *not* offer the MMCD did experience some deposit erosion.) The answer to the second part of the question, although not quite as easy, is somewhat predictable. The depositors who were attracted to the MMCD were interest sensitive and had fairly high balances. In other words, they behaved like the economist's "rational man" theory suggested they might. And it is likely that these depositors will continue to behave predictably. They are interested in both *rate* and *liquidity* (rate alone is not enough, or the money would already have been in higher yielding uses). It is expected that as money market rates fall, the funds will either stay where they are (in the decreasingly yielding MMCs) or find their way back into liquid accounts. Some may take refuge in longer term deposits, but since this was not their origin, one would guess that liquidity will again play a role in the depositor's assessment.

Since so many of the MMCD deposits come from existing deposit bases, bankers put forth the argument that they have to offer them. There is probably some merit to this proposition. These deposits were originally core deposits; and as we move toward the elimination of Regulation Q, it is likely that more of our deposits will have highly variable cost components like the MMCD.

The real lesson of the MMCD is that we must not only *increase* our *asset yields* to allow for such funding fluctuations, but we must endeavor to develop more flexibility in our asset yields. As deposit rates of interest become increasingly variable, so must our asset rates of interest. Mortgage loans, consumer loans, and other term-type loans must be either priced high enough to accommodate anticipated fluctuations in funding costs or priced on a variable rate basis.

Now, no bank wants to merely break even (or have all the profits come from a handful of high DDA balance customers). We're moving toward an era when *all* depositors should contribute to a bank's bottom line. And this means, in theory, a profit margin should be built into our cost of funds as we calculate our minimum deposit sizes.

Let's say that we want to earn 1% on average assets. And that this becomes our target profit. The question, then, becomes how much do we need to mark-up each source of funds to achieve this goal; and what minimum deposit size will result?

The following equation can be helpful in relating your assets to earning assets to deposits.

$$\begin{array}{c}\text{Profit Spread}\\\text{over Cost of}\\\text{Deposit}\end{array} = \dfrac{\text{Target Return on Average Assets}}{\dfrac{\text{Average Earning}}{\text{Assets}} \div \dfrac{\text{Average Total}}{\text{Assets}}} \div \dfrac{\dfrac{\text{Average Total}}{\text{Deposits}}}{\dfrac{\text{Average Earning}}{\text{Assets}}}$$

This equation takes the desired return on average assets and first modifies it by the relationship between total and earning assets. Obviously, if a bank has a low proportion of earning assets to total assets, each earning asset must contribute that much more if the profit goal is to be realized. This figure is then modified by the ratio of total deposits to earning assets, since it is deposits that we are marking up.

Example

Let's say you are a bank with the following:

$55 million average total assets*
$52 million average total deposits*
$50 million average earning assets*
1.00% target return on average assets
*Projected for year

This equation then suggests that you should mark-up your deposit costs by 1.058%:

$$1.058\% = \frac{1.00\%}{50 \text{ million} \div 55 \text{ million}} \div \frac{52 \text{ million}}{50 \text{ million}}$$

In other words, if you want to earn 1.00% on average assets ($550,000), you've got to earn 1.05% on average deposits, after operating costs have been recovered.

Apply this concept to pricing a six-month MMCD; let's say the published maximum rate you can pay is 13%. Based upon the calculations above, you need to add in another 1.058% profit to meet your return in assets (ROA) goal of 1.00%. And, of course, you must also cover the $13.16 annualized operating costs (see Table 3.4). This means you need a spread of 1.57%:

.52%   (to cover operating costs) plus
1.05%   (to provide profit)
―――――
1.57%   (rounds to 1.19%)

Add this to your interest cost of 13% and you need to invest this money in an asset whose net yield exceeds 14.57% (13% + 1.57%).

A convenient equation for such a pricing decision would be:

$$\frac{\text{Annualized Operating Costs}}{\text{Net Matched Asset Yield} - (\text{Interest Cost} + \text{Mark Up})} = \frac{\text{Minimum}}{\text{Balance}}$$

Should any one of the elements in this formula be absent or under review, it can be determined by algebraic means.

The Pricing of Savings Accounts vs. Certificates

There is a significant difference between the application of these pricing concepts to regular passbook savings accounts versus some of the higher balance certificates.

For the most part, regular passbook savings accounts appeal to the mass market, while certificates appeal more to the older, more affluent segment of the market. In general the mass market is much less rate sensitive than the older, higher balance segment. Consequently, the pricing emphasis differs.

With regular savings accounts, the pricing focus is on the minimum balance and any fee that might be levied should that balance level be violated. With certificates, especially money market-type certificates, the focus is less on the minimum balance and more on the interest rates and related interest margins.

Of course, this does not mean that the minimum balances associated with certificates are unimportant, since the minimum balance more than any other variable determines who is eligible for the product. The point is, higher rate certificates should be limited to those whose balances are sufficiently large to offset the annualized operating costs with a much lower interest margin.

ACCOUNT BASE PROFITABILITY

It is easy enough for a bank to adjust the minimum balances required for its various certificates. If you feel yours are too low, simply change your rules and begin issuing all new CDs with the new minimums. When existing CDs below your new minimum mature and prior experience leads customers to believe they'll be "rolled over," you have a few choices:

- Send them a check with a letter explaining your new rules
- Roll them over into regular savings with a letter explaining the new rules

I'd recommend the latter approach, since it has the effect of maintaining the deposits in the bank.

While the issue of adjusting CD minimums is fairly straightforward, the questions surrounding the issue of changing regular savings conditions is more complex. FCA studies show that in the typical middle-sized bank ($50 to $200 million) over 40% of these accounts maintain balances of less than $100. This fact produces a condition not unlike that of the low balance checking account — a lot of activity costs with little offsetting revenue from balances. During 1981 and 1982, bankers began to recognize this and improved their profits significantly by imposing charges on lower balance savings accounts.

Just for the fun of it, let's take a look at some of the hidden profit potential in these low balance savings accounts. To give you a feel for where we are going, I'll make a few assumptions and push through some calculations. Then I'll give you a sampling and analysis format that you can implement in your bank.

Hidden Profit Potential — Example Data

Let's say our bank has 13,000 regular savings accounts; and that these accounts represent $60 million in deposits. If this bank is like most, 41% of these accounts will be under $100 in balances. These 5,330 will represent a very small proportion of total deposits (less than 1%), but account for at least 41% of total costs and probably more, since low balance savings accounts usually exhibit higher activity.

It is clear that with the following FCA costs a savings balance of $100 is inadequate.

Annual Maintenance	$14.14
Cost Per Deposit	$ .56
Cost Per Withdrawal	$ 1.09
4 Annual Interest Postings	$ 7.92 ($1.98 each)

The net interest margin on $100 is $5.13 per year (assume net yield of 10.52% and 5.39% interest cost). Assuming that a typical low balance customer makes 5 deposits and 4 withdrawals annually, our bank is $25.07 in the hole, annually (or $6.02 quarterly).

Costs

Maintenance	$14.14
Open/Close Account	$ .98
5 Deposits	$ 2.80
4 Withdrawals	$ 4.36
4 Interest Postings	$ 7.92
	$30.20

Revenue

Interest Income (10.52%)	$10.52
Interest Expense (5.39%)	$ 5.39
Net Interest Margin	$ 5.13

This is probably a conservative figure, since lower balance accounts generally do exhibit greater activity. Nevertheless, with an annual operating loss of $25.07, these 5,330 accounts represent a significant hidden profit potential. As we'll see, there are a couple of factors that will reduce the amount of this potential which is realizable, but even the residual will be very attractive.

Account Base Profitability

One factor mitigating our ability to recapture all of these costs is the likelihood that some of these low balance savings customers may have profitable checking accounts (or other services). And since our operating (data processing) state of the art does not yet permit "total relationship pricing," we may want to go slowly toward the recovery of savings account losses. (More will be said a little later on how to evaluate the account base profitability factor).

Reprice Low Balance Savings

In spite of these two factors, we should reprice our low balance savings accounts. But carefully. Let's return to our example. Let's say that we decide not to pay interest on any account whose average balance is below $100.

NOTE: Checking accounts were priced on the basis of *minimums* for purposes of simplicity and maximum profits. Since there is no payment of interest, consumers opt for simplicity of understanding given widely fluctuating balances. Savings accounts do pay interest and are much less volatile; and since we need savings deposits, we favor the more equitable method of recognizing average balances.

If our 5,330 accounts having less than $100 average $26, then the elimination of interest will save our bank $7,469 (5,330 × $26 × .0539) in annual interest expense, if no accounts close. If some accounts close, we'll also be saving the associated operating costs.

TABLE 3.5 Annual Savings Resulting from Not Paying Interest on Savings Accounts with Less Than $100.

% of Accounts Closing	Annual Interest Savings[1]	Annual Operating Savings[2]	Annual Revenue Lost[3]	Annual Net
0	$7,469	0	0	$ 7,469
10	$7,469	$16,096	$1,457	$ 7,469
20	$7,469	$32,193	$2,915	$36,747
50	$7,469	$80,483	$7,289	$80,663

[1] Assumes only those affected leave
[2] $30.20 per account
[3] 10.52% net yield and $26 average balance

It is easy to see that the annual operating savings dwarfs the annual interest savings; and that the bank is really better off without these accounts.

Quarterly Fee

In fact, some banks have decided that the profit potential associated with eliminating (or neutralizing) low balance accounts is so great that they have installed explicit fees on low balance accounts. Let's say we charge a quarterly fee of $2.00 on each account whose average balance is below $100 (as well as not pay interest).

TABLE 3.6 Increase in Annual Profitability of Savings Accounts Resulting from Pricing Accounts with Less Than $100.

% of Accounts Closing	Annual Interest Savings	Annual Operating Savings	Annual Interest Revenue Lost	Fee Income	Net
0	$7,469	$0	$0	$42,640	$ 49,569
10	$7,469	$16,096	$1,457	$38,376	$ 60,484
20	$7,469	$32,193	$2,915	$34,112	$ 70,859
40	$7,469	$64,386	$5,831	$25,584	$ 92,608
50	$7,469	$80,483	$7,289	$21,320	$101,983

Incremental Costs

One question which will undoubtedly come to mind is whether this bank would actually save $32,193 in operating costs if 20% of its savings account base closed their accounts.

The answer is probably not. Studies of specific banks done by Whittle, Raddon, Motley & Hanks, Inc. using Functional Cost Analysis data suggest that anywhere from 40% to 60% of the annual operating costs of a savings account are for overhead items such as occupancy expense, executive salaries, etc. Nevertheless, if our example bank lost 20% of its base, it would still save $12,877 (40% × $32,193) in operating costs even if overhead were 60% of the $30.20 annualized operating costs.

But this is not the key figure in this analysis, since with a pricing program of $2.00 per quarter on each account below $100, the bank would generate fee income of $34,112 per year until the accounts were liquidated.

At that point the incremental savings would be $64,386 (5,330 × $30.20 × 40%) and with 5,330 fewer accounts, one would also expect some reduction in overhead.

Because this price of $2.00 is still below cost ($30.20 per account per year = $7.55/quarter), the bank still maximizes short-term profits if all accounts leave the bank. In fact, if we were to ignore historic pricing patterns and the effect of affiliated business, the best pricing structure from a theoretical point of view would be one that extracted explicit fees equivalent to the annual loss.

TABLE 3.7   Quarterly Loss on Small Savings Accounts

Average Balance	Annual Operating Cost ($)	Net Interest Margin*	Annual Loss ÷ 4
0–100	$30.20	$ 2.56	$6.91
101–500	$30.20	$15.39	$3.70
501–1,000	$30.20	$38.47	None

*Assumes mid-range balance — yield 10.52%, interest 5.39%.

Such an analysis might lead to the pricing structure as shown in table 3.8, if the rough edges were smoothed over.

Customers in the mid-range are given a somewhat better deal under the theory that they are more nearly profitable and, not being children, are more likely to have associated business.

TABLE 3.8   Pricing Structure of Savings Accounts

Average Savings Balance	Quarterly Fee
0–100	$6.00
101–500	$4.00
+500	0

Timing

Even though this pricing structure is cost justified, it would be inappropriate for a bank inaugurating savings pricing for the very first time. Experience in consulting with banks on the subject of savings pricing suggests the applicability of the old Chinese proverb, "Even the longest journey begins with but a single step."

The initial effort to recapture savings account costs should probably occur at the $100 and below level. The Functional Cost Analysis studies reveal that over 41% of all savings accounts have less than $100 in them; and that these accounts represent less than 1% of all regular savings deposits.

Why so many small accounts? Probably because of a couple of factors. First, many customers over the years tried to close their accounts, but were instructed by bank employees to "keep just one dollar in the account" in order to receive interest. Other causes of very small accounts are the popular premium programs and other promotional plays designed to encourage people to open small accounts. The point is, though, that if you start out your savings pricing effort at a low minimum you will solve the greatest portion of your problem with very little public relations backlash.

Sampling Your Customer Base

This analysis looks only at the profit dynamics of the regular savings base. But if you are a commercial bank, your principal deposit service (from a marketing if not a profit point of view) is the checking account. If many of your low balance savers have a checking account that is

TABLE 3.9   Regular Savings Account — Frequency Distribution &
Cross-Sell

	1.	2.	3.	4.	5.	6.
Average Balance	# in Sample	% in Sample	Median Balance ($)	Mean Balance ($)	Median Annual Deposits Made	Median Annual Withdrawals Made
0– 25	163	25	12	8	12	10
26– 50	65	10	32	40	8	8
51– 100	39	6	78	81	5	4
101– 500	65	10	210	381	8	6
501– 1,000	78	12	691	702	6	3
1,001– 5,000	85	13	2,450	3,895	2	1
5,001–10,000	98	15	7,502	7,200	1	0
+10,000	59	9	19,448	32,800	1	0
TOTAL	651	100			6.12	4.63

profitable or if they use other services to a significant degree, then perhaps we cannot be so aggressive in our savings loss recovery program.

We know from the checking profile and from market research studies that the potential cross-usage of such non-checking services as CDs, installment loans, mortgages, and bank cards is too low generally, to warrant underpriced core deposit services (i.e., checking, savings), but it is possible that we've done a great job in cross-selling checking; and that by virtue of their combined profitability we do *not* need to impose either interest payment restrictions or service fees. To get a feel for this, you should take a random sample of your savings base and collect data on *average balances, activity, and other services used.* This data can be arrayed like that in Table 3.9.

TABLE 3.9   Regular Savings Account — Frequency Distribution & Cross-Sell (continued)

7.	8.	9.	10.	11.	12.	13.
			Cross Selling			
% DDA	*DDA Median Balance*	*% CD*	*% Installment*	*% Mortgage*	*% Bank Card*	*% Overdraft Credit*
8	198	0	10	2	14	5
5	175	1	13	0	18	4
10	251	4	15	1	21	2
15	151	3	18	5	35	5
20	295	5	24	8	41	8
28	310	5	18	11	50	10
31	341	8	15	10	51	8
36	385	10	12	5	41	12
18.5		4	15	5	33	7

SAVINGS ACCOUNT PROFILE

The following forms, instructions, and calculation definitions should help you complete your own savings account profile like the one discussed in Table 3.9.

Form I: Regular Savings Account Profile Form

This form is to be completed on each of a sampling of your regular savings accounts. If you have more than one type of regular savings account, test each separately. A description of sampling procedures follows the form.

REGULAR SAVINGS ACCOUNT PROFILE

Last Name _____ Savings Account # _____

1. Average savings account balance $ _____
   (whole dollars only)
2. Annual deposits made   _____
3. Annual withdrawals made   _____
4. Annual service charge on savings $ _____
5. Checking account?
   1-yes   2-no   (Skip to Q. #9)
6. Average checking balances $ _____
   (whole dollars only)
7. Average annual checking transactions   _____
   (Debits)
8. Annual charge on checking $ _____
9. CD
   1-yes   2-no
10. Installment loan
    1-yes   2-no
11. Mortage
    1-yes   2-no
12. Bank charge card
    1-yes   2-no
13. Overdraft credit
    1-yes   2-no

Note to User: Right justify all fields

SAVINGS ACCOUNT PROFILE
DATA COLLECTION

The Regular Savings Account Profile represents your master data collection form designed for gathering sample information. Based upon the sample size (see below) you'll have to duplicate the master form. If you have more than one savings account type, type the name of each plan in the upper right hand corner of the master before duplicating it, and use different color paper, if possible.

Random Sampling Procedure

To achieve a true random sample, simply divide the desired sample size into the total number in the base, and then take every Nth name as a unit in the sample where:

$$N = \frac{\text{Total Account Base}}{\text{Sample Size}}$$

Example: If there are 4,000 savings accounts and 400 is the desired sample size, then divide 400 into 4,000 to produce 10. Therefore, every 10th savings account is included.

Sample Size

Sample size is very important but it is not a constant percentage. The larger the number of accounts in a base, the lower the percent sample required.

Account Base	Sample Size
Under 3,000	300
3,001–5,000	10%
5,001–10,000	7%
10,001–20,000	5%
Over 20,000	2.5%

Collecting and Recording Data

1. Average Savings Account Balance
   It is preferable that this figure be a 12 month average. However, if your files are not set up this way, a one month average is acceptable. Indicate in whole dollars the average balance in the account.
   Example: $ 5,925

2. Annual Deposits Made
   If you're using monthly data, multiply by 12 to provide annual data.
   Example: 3 per month × 12 =   36

3. Annual Withdrawals Made
   Same as question 2.

4. Annual Service Charge on Savings
   If you do not charge on savings accounts, leave blank. Otherwise, same procedure as question 2.

5. Checking Account
   Check the DDA file to determine whether the account name also has a checking account. Circle 1-Yes or 2-No. If No, go to question 9.

6. Average Checking Balance
   As in question 1, a 12 month average is preferred, but a representative one month figure is acceptable. Use whole dollars only.
   Example: $ 482

7. Average Annual Checking Transactions
   As in question 2, if you're using monthly data, multiply by 12 to provide annual data.
   Example: 15 per month × 12 = 180

8. Annual Charge on Checking
   Use only whole dollars. Round to nearest whole dollars. If you are working with monthly data, multiply by 12.

9. Simply indicate whether the account name also has at least one of the indicated services.

PRICING STRATEGY, STRUCTURE AND SAVINGS ACCOUNT IMPLEMENTATION

Micro-economists will tell you that costs are not relevant in setting price. The foregoing analysis which defines what a bank can gain by losing customers dispells this concept, particularly when one understands that in banking we have a two-dimensional pricing structure (fees or balances) which enables us to maintain two alternate prices.

Costs are not irrelevant, they are pivotal to the pricing question. Generally, in fact, the pricing goal in the near term is to recapture or eliminate these costs. But consumer behavior and what economists would call "demand characteristics" are also important — not so much because they will influence the pricing decision itself, but because they will influence *how* it is carried out. As we learned in the previous chapter on checking accounts, consumers are sensitive to the way charges are made as well as to the level of the charge.

Market Research

With this in mind, it is helpful to review some of the basic consumer behavior influences of savings/time product pricing. This data extracted from the studies done by Whittle, Raddon, Motley & Hanks, Inc., is offered as general background to the following discussion of pricing structure. Determination should be based on the applicability of the data to your local market.

Consumers Feel Entitled to Interest

Focus groups among potential users of NOW accounts reveal that most people would rather earn a full rate on balances *and* pay a fee than earn a lesser rate even when in reality the lower rate is a better deal. The reason is that consumers react emotionally to the idea that the bank is using their money and since most people lack the financial acuity to make the judgment accurate, they assume the higher rate is a better deal.

Generally speaking, then, it is as easy to charge a fee of $8.00 a year ($2.00 per quarter) as it is to eliminate the payment of $2.63 in interest ($50 × 5.25%). Moreover, charging a fee for service and giving full market value for deposits is, in theory, more in tune with the evolutionary direction of deposit service pricing.

Some Consumers Feel Obligated To Behave Rationally

Some people, particularly those who are older, and more affluent, feel an obligation to behave in their own best interests even when the cost/benefit analysis suggests that the action is not all that worthwhile. For example, most people keep their savings account at a thrift to earn ¼% more interest. Recognizing that the average consumer has about $3,000 in savings, the additional $7.50 per year hardly seems worth the additional time, gasoline, and hassle. But many people don't see it that way. They feel an obligation to behave rationally and will do almost anything to get their full return.

People Are Financially Lazy

This is a corollary to the principle above. Some people are very picky and will travel to the ends of the earth for ¼% more interest; others couldn't care less. In 1973, when Regulation Q changed, many banks ingeniously offered a "new savings plan" (e.g., statement) paying 5%, as well as the "old passbook" paying 4½%. And to their surprise (or predictably!) many, if not most, of the 4½% people did not change their accounts.

The 80/20 Rule

Eighty per cent (or more) of your consumer deposits are provided by as few as 20% of your customers. Generally, these people tend to be more interest sensitive and will move their money to the better deal. The success of the money market CD lends credence to this rule. These depositors offer the most compelling reason for bankers to stay alert to regulatory changes and for offering some version of the permissible new services.

But the other 80% of your customers who account for only 20% of your deposits argue for a segmented marketing effort. You should not simply change your existing products so that all depositors obtain the higher rate, interest on checkings, or whatever. This 80% of your customers account for over 80% of your costs and they do not have the balances to pay for the more costly product enhancements.

And just as important, many of them are simply not that attuned to the benefit of the enhancement; and, due to this apathy or ignorance, are just as happy to stay where they are.

Consumers Learn More During Each Inflation

In 1977, the consuming public probably never heard of a T-bill. By 1978, one year later, financial institutions had over $100 billion of "T-bill related" deposits. During each period of high interest rates, competition for scarce funds increases; and the 20% of customers who provide 80% of deposits learn where to put their money. They are generally conservative and value liquidity; but within an acceptable maturity range, they will seek the best return.

Savings Accounts Are Secondary Services

Research done by Whittle, Raddon, Motley & Hanks, Inc. in various markets around the country and in nationwide surveys consistently shows that people do business with more than one type of financial institution. In fact, the average is between two and three types per family. An example would be a family who has a checking account at the local bank; a savings account at the local thrift; and an auto loan at a credit union.

Research also shows that the checking relationship determines the primary relationship. And it is very difficult to get people to switch primary banks. A savings relationship is not as convenience dominated and forms the principal service defining the secondary relationship. If properly motivated, as in a premium program, people will move a savings account.

Working People Are An Excellent Source Of Funds

Banks located near well-paying, heavy industry complexes often have substantial core savings deposits; and, as a result, enjoy a fairly low cost source of funds. Generally, working families in the +40 age group are providers of deposits.

They don't feel comfortable using brokerage firm services and show less inclination to move funds around in response to interest rate changes.

Premiums Work

Offering merchandise premiums is an effective way to attract savings deposits. Some people may not be financially sophisticated insofar as disintermediating funds is concerned, but there is a market that has demonstrated a sensitivity to merchandise premiums.

Very often, it is a minority of people that responds to various competitor offerings; and to this extent the increase in deposits can be illusory, since these same people may go down the street next quarter, if the premium is better.

NOTE: Premiums are like trading stamps. They are easy to duplicate; and once you've started them in your market, they are hard to stop.

Premium Minimums Determine Participation More Than Deposit Size

Generally, the premium minimum balance, rather than the amount of the average deposit, will influence the number of people who will participate. Many people will simply move their entire savings account, but are more inclined to participate if the minimum is low. The reason reflects their concern of deposit liquidity. Often they believe they are obligated to keep the minimum required deposit in the bank for an extended period of time.

Premium Respondents Are Limited And Fickle

The people who activate on premiums are a fairly limited group and are often characterized as "premium junkies." They will activate on one premium after another and show little loyalty. If you are in the premium business, you have two ways to satisfy these customers:

- Always come up with the best premium
- Offer a continuing premium (e.g. Saver's Club or Saver's Magazine with continuing premiums)

Savings Are Sacred

When asked to evaluate the various new payment and funds transfer mechanisms (e.g., NOW accounts, telephone transfer, automatic transfer), consumers let it be known that they did not like the idea of the bank fooling with their savings accounts. Some consumers in New England have both a NOW account (i.e., draftable savings) and a savings account. They perceive the NOW as a checking account not as a savings account. Most Automatic Transfer Service (ATS), Savings-to-Checking, programs were, in reality, zero balance checking accounts paying interest.

NOTE: Consumers are deal oriented and love the idea of getting something free; hence the success of the various programs designed to eliminate checking charges for savings balances.

Savings & Loans "Own" The Savers Market Position

Over 95% of America's families have checking accounts and savings accounts. The vast majority have their checking acount at a bank, but their principal savings account at a thrift. It is likely that in your market and among your customers two thirds (67%) will have their largest savings account at a thrift. A comparison of Federal Reserve and FHLB data showed that the median savings balance at a thrift is also double that at a commercial bank.

In-depth studies of savers reveal that in addition to offering a higher rate of interest, thrifts have the advantage of being perceived as a place for the average man or woman. This means that thrifts have effectively positioned themselves for the average family and do not project the cold, impersonal, and big business image that their competitor commercial banks do.

NOTE: The image a bank projects often has little to do with the real desire of the bank's CEO and staff. In all our studies of community banks, few actually want to project the "cool, for business only" image. Nevertheless, this is often how they are seen.

Basic Pricing Strategy

Based upon the foregoing analysis and that presented earlier in the book, it is our belief that the best pricing strategy for consumer savings/time services is the following: *Set economic minimum balances and aggressively seek all conforming deposits, particularly from among your own customer base and "funds providing" segments of the market.*

The engagement of this strategy requires two distinctly different, yet related programs. First, you must police low-balance accounts. You should give them every opportunity to become economically viable, but on a phased basis to minimize the loss of profitable accounts. Secondly, you must devise added incentives for new and existing customers to bring you even *more* of their total deposit relationship.

Let's look at these programs a little more closely.

Set Economically Viable Minimum Balances

As has already been discussed, the following are breakeven balances and related operating guidelines for the various savings/time accounts (assuming daily compounding).

Factors To Consider in Choosing Your Minimum/Fees

Emotionalism

Although people object to checking service charges, they *do* recognize the service component of this product, and will pay for it. Great progress has been made in the past few years in convincing people that checking accounts are a service for which a price is justifiable.

A savings account is different. It is perceived by consumers as "money set aside, earning interest for a rainy day." They are less likely to recognize the service component, because savings deposits are not involved in the payments system. Also, they can get this service at many more competing institutions. All this together means that there is much greater potential for loss of accounts.

The pricing structure presented here considers this, and is conservative; the minimums are generally below breakeven. This pricing strategy recognizes the short-term priority banks should place on attracting their existing customer's savings deposits. Nevertheless, it will represent significant increases in many cases. There is, however, potential for loss of accounts. In fact, your minimums should be set with the *expectation* that you'll lose many of the accounts under your minimums. This is why the cost analysis is important.

Lower Balance Accounts

The aggressiveness of your savings pricing should relate to the number of low balance accounts. For example, if you have a lot of low balance accounts providing little associated business, you should price high and not worry if you lose them.

This high price should be communicated within the context that customers should combine savings deposits to get greater value; e.g., "saver's club" ($2,000 minimum) combined with a hard-hitting campaign to show the value of various non-interest product features. This will give the potentially profitable customers a stronger reason to bring you more money. But you must recognize that many will simply not have the money and will leave. View this as exporting earnings problems.

The following is offered as a rule of thumb in the pricing of regular savings accounts. The key factor is the percentage of accounts under $100 from your account profile.

TABLE 3.10   Guidelines for Pricing Regular Savings Accounts.

% of Accounts Under $100	Action
0–10	Be careful; let sleeping dogs lie. Potential loss of high balance; impose $50 minimum opening balances on new accounts. Limit withdrawals.
10–25	Impose minimum operating balance of $100. Don't pay interest on balances of under $100. Limit withdrawals.
+25	Quarterly fee and no interest on balance of under $100. Limit withdrawals. Minimum opening balance.

New certificates of deposit should simply conform to the suggested minimums, since by definition lower deposits are not profitable (unless your net yield is significantly higher).

DEPOSIT SERVICE PRODUCT DEVELOPMENT

The principal impetus to savings product development comes from Washington as regulators seek better ways to achieve the often conflicting goals of banks, consumers, and economists. Based upon current trends, it is clear that there is a desire for banks to pay higher rates of interest on smaller and smaller deposits. Of necessity, this will result in the following product development responses by banks.

Explicit Fees for Service (plus other revenue enhancers)
If banks are permitted (or forced) to pay money market rates for deposits, they must not only increase their loan rates and make them more interest-sensitive, they must also charge explicit fees for deposit services. They *must* do both. Increasing and varying loan rates alone is not enough, since most depositors don't use loans and the result would be inequitable. To only impose deposit service fees is not enough because the bank's principal earning asset base must be changed to reflect more adequately its principal cost base — i.e., asset price should reflect liability costs.

Product Differentiation
As banks are permitted to increase rates and/or offer new, more attractive deposit services, attention must be paid to the cost of various operating methods.

The desire to maintain low interest costs on passbook savings while remaining competitive may argue for the introduction of a new savings plan (e.g., statement savings) which pays higher rates or compounds in a better way or pays interest from day-of-deposit to day-of-withdrawal. Many customers will be attracted to this differentiated service. Others will stay with the passbook. You must weigh the incremental operating costs against:

- the incremental deposits attracted to the bank
- the deposits preserved in a lower-cost product as a result of not converting everyone to the higher cost

War Bonds (Discount Note)

One alternative bankers have discussed as a way to compete for the interest-sensitive low balance savings market is through the issuance of discounted bonds that mature. These still have associated costs which might be *estimated* to be as low as:

Open Account	$1.00
Close Account	$1.00
Account Maintenance	$2.00

Given these costs, relevant annualized costs for the various maturities would be:

1 year	$4.00
2½ years	$2.80
4 years	$2.50

And assuming daily interest compounding and a net interest margin of 2.00%, breakeven minimums would be $200 for 1 year, $140 for 2½ years, and $125 for 4 years.

Again, under the theory that we have to be competitive, yet make money, you might consider a war bond plan where customers could choose one to four year maturities for $500.

Practice Market Segmentation
Market segmentation is related to product differentiation. Not everyone is interest-rate sensitive. In fact, there is evidence to suggest that only the 20% of depositors who provide 80% of deposits are. The other 80% are less interest sensitive, but

account for well over a majority of the operating costs. This basic economic fact argues for the "stick and carrot" approach to developing and pricing new deposit services. Develop and offer newly differentiated savings services using different operating methods. Make the features of the service very attractive. Then price it and its "substitute" to maximize profits.

Example (Regular Savings)

- Regular 5¼% passbook
  5¼% interest compounded quarterly
- Saver's bonus 5½% account
  5½% compounded daily
  Statement savings (single statement with checking)
  Over $2,000 qualifies customer as member of Saver's Club

Such a dichotomy would serve to attract existing customers who are rate sensitive, while maintaining the lower costs among customers loyal to passbooks.

Communicating New Deposit Minimums to Existing Customers

After you have done your analysis and developed your new deposit minimums, you must consider how to communicate these minimums to existing as well as to new customers. We'll return to the question of attracting new customers later, but for now let's focus on communicating with existing customers. There are essentially three communications media you should consider:

- In-lobby communications
- Mail/statement stuffers
- Employees (training)

Before we examine each of these in detail, it's important to understand the potential for losing accounts. As explained earlier, it is highly likely that you'll encounter more price sensitivity on savings than on checking. And as suggested, your pricing should be structured with the anticipation that you'll lose a significant portion of those under the minimums. Given this expectation, your communications job is to convince everyone (those affected as well as those not affected) to meet and even exceed your minimums.

1. *In-Lobby Communications*
   There is a confusing array of alternative savings concepts from which your customers have to choose. They view their investment decision as important, but difficult. And they want help. They see your staff as a group of well-trained professionals possessing the expertise to help simplify this decision. In fact, in the evolving deregulated market for financial services, this face-to-face proximity is one of your greatest advantages.

2. *Mail/Statement Stuffers*
   If you are changing your minimums, you'll want to communicate this to existing customers. You can either send a first-class letter to everyone at the same time or stuff the announcement in your statement (if you have one).
   NOTE: Be sure to check your signature card on any non-maturing account to make sure you have not contractually obligated yourself to specific pricing conditions. If you have, you may have no alternative but to offer a differentiated service.
   You should try to couple your new minimums with a new service offering under the "good news/bad news" concept. An example of such a letter is shown in Exhibit 6.

EXHIBIT 6   Letter Offering New Service.

Dear Saver:

It is our desire here at National Bank to give our depositors the maximum value for their deposit dollar. We know this is especially important in these times of high inflation.

New Service
So we are pleased to announce our new "First Saver's Club" which pays 5.25% (5.39% annual yield). This new interest rate is higher than that available on regular passbook savings. And, in addition, our First Saver's Club Members get:

- Free Checking
- Merchandise Discounts
- Travel Discounts
- VSP (Very Special People) Service

What's more, you'll earn interest from day of deposit 'til day of withdrawal. These are big advantages and we invite everyone to join our First Saver's Club. With advantages like these, it's now smarter to keep *all* your savings at one place — here in a First Saver's Club Account!

Of course, we have many other savings plans designed for various savings needs. Effective immediately, the following savings plans and terms are available from National Bank:

MENU OF RATES

So please stop in and let us help you decide which plan is best for you. Or give me a call at XXX-XXXX.

Mary Jones
National Bank

If you cannot use the "good news/bad news" approach and feel you must own up to your new pricing schedule, consider a letter like the one in Exhibit 7.

EXHIBIT 7   Letter Informing Customers of New Pricing Schedule.

Dear Saver:

It is our desire to continue to give our depositors maximum value for their deposit dollars. And we are constantly reviewing our accounts to see how we can better achieve this goal.

Recently, we discovered that many of our regular savings accounts have balances of under $100. These accounts are very costly to our bank and limit our ability to give even greater value for deposit dollars. To ensure that our customers continue to receive an excellent return on their deposit dollar, we have found it necessary to adjust our savings account minimum balances.

Savings Programs

Effective immediately, the following savings programs will be available at National Bank.

MENU OF RATES

CD Below Minimum

If you currently have a Certificate of Deposit below these minimums, upon maturity these funds will be transferred to a regular savings account.

Bring Us All Your Deposits

We hope that you find our banking facilities convenient, and our employees friendly and accommodating. And we hope you'll consider bringing us all of your savings deposits.

Sincerely,

Mary Jones
National Bank

---

3. *Employee Training*

Recognizing that your new accounts people and platform officers turnover frequently and are not often as well trained as your customers think, you should place an "Investments Menu" board at each new accounts desk and at other strategically located places in your lobby. This menu board should outline the various savings plans and their features as well as some brief commentary regarding the use to which each is best put. The menu should be reproduced in an "Investment Plans" brochure for customers to take home.

- *Sales Training*
  Break the new accounts people up into small groups. Have them practice answering objections and selling in a role-playing environment. Get them involved.
- *Product Education*
  Put your menu board and/or brochure into an Employee Information Kit and give one to each employee. Conduct pop quizzes on details during the week and give employees small rewards if they answer correctly.

Timing

Allow yourself sufficient time for effective implementation. The biggest problems arise when banks try to hurry up to get one more month's improved revenue. Consider the following schedule.

Price Adjustment Schedule

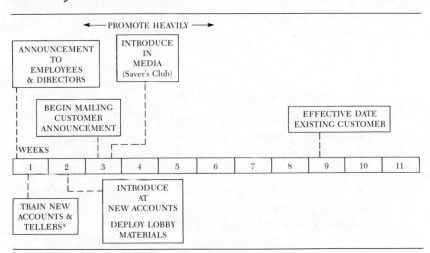

*Depending on branch distribution, an additional week of training may be necessary.

The Grandmother Syndrome

The only grey lining in the silver cloud of eliminating low balance savings accounts is the chance that you might also eliminate the sponsor of one of these accounts, whose deposits total $40,000! There are alternative ways to prevent this:

- Have grandma put the minimum in her grandchild's account.
- Pay interest on any low balance savings account sponsored by another higher balance account.
- Develop and offer a special "Youngster's Savings Club" to the children of your customers.

Good Communication with Employees

The single most important communications tool you have is your own employees. Take great pains to sell them on your new pricing structure and make sure they can all explain it. Here are some guidelines to follow.

Employee Presentation
Get all your employees together and go through your account profile. Show them how much an account costs; and how it breaks even. Tell them where their salaries come from and how loss accounts compromise these. Talk about the fact that most people keep money at other banks or financial institutions; and that you want to convince people to do more of their business with your bank. Don't talk down to them — they are smart. It's just that no one usually takes the time to explain banking to them.

Attracting New Higher Balance Accounts

The previous discussion relates primarily to regulating or eliminating low balance accounts. Some of you, for a variety of good reasons, will elect not to take this difficult step. But you'll still want to improve your average balance size. This means you've got to assume an offensive posture. Like pushing on a rope, it is harder to achieve as dramatic a set of results as come with eliminating low balance accounts, but it is, nevertheless, vital if commercial banks are to be viable competitors in the marketplace for consumer deposits.

The Problems

There are two very real, tangible problems that banks must overcome if they are to attract new high balance savings accounts.

1. ¼% Interest Differential
    Even though this amounts to only $2.50 per year per $1,000, people think it's important. In fact, research reveals that one-quarter of the people asked thought it was worth over $25 per year per $1,000!
    To overcome this disadvantage, you need to offer a better deal. And the deal has to be perceptibly better and it cannot be interest.
2. "Not for the Little Guy" Image
    Banks are seen as places for rich businessmen, lawyers, doctors — not for the average working woman or man, yet it is these people who save. Research shows that the two great consumer market segments that provide funds are senior citizens and working class families over age 45 and that they actually feel more comfortable at a thrift.

These two problems must be overcome. You, your marketing staff, and your ad agency should devote the highest possible priority to this problem. And here are some ideas to consider.

Problem #1 — Overcome the ¼% Interest Advantage

Take your Account Profile, and any market research you have, lock yourself in a room and chew on these product alternatives.

Saver's Club
$2,000 to $5,000 in regular savings gets you:

- free checking
- merchandise discounts at local stores
- travel discounts
- newsletter

Free Checking for High Balance Savers
If you don't want or can't afford the Saver's Club, reduce the cost of your checking for savings dollars. If you reduce the fee $1.00 per month for $1,000 in savings, this is $12.00 per year and well above the $2.50 interest differential.

Merchandise Premiums
Run periodic merchandise premiums (quarterly). Use brand name merchandise that has well known value so that your deal is easily seen.

Investors Newsletter
Affiliate with any one of a number of national publishers producing a financially-oriented newsletter which contains not only good articles but *merchandise* and *travel* offers. This is similar to the Saver's Club but without the hassle.

Investment Seminars
Take advantage of your professional image and hold seminars on better personal money management designed to take the mystery out of the increasingly confusing savings/ investment array of alternatives.

There are undoubtedly other product packages or alternatives that you might use. The key is to position what you develop as a better deal. This is why the depositor took his or her money to another financial institution; and it's the way you must get it back.

Problem #2 — Reposition Your Image

You must "position" your bank in the mind of your market and in so doing "reposition" your competitor. In New York State, the mutual savings banks developed a statewide joint positioning program designed to establish themselves as "banks for people" and commercial banks as "banks for business." This concept was very effective and the commercial bankers retaliated by saying in the media, "come to us when you want more than just a friend." In other words, the bank counterattacked the friendliness position with the professionalism position. Positioning is basically taking advantage of your competitors weakness under the theory that for every strength there is a corollary weakness.

Right now, thrifts own the savings position. And you've got to develop a positioning strategy which amplifies your strengths, their weaknesses, and substitutes your bank in the consumer's mind as "the savings place." The key to this is your professionalism and the fact that you're the primary financial institution as determined by either convenience or reputation.

Again, you should meet with your marketing staff and/or agency to review these key considerations of an effective positioning program.

MONEY MARKET ACCOUNTS

During the fall of 1982 major legislative and regulatory actions brought about the creation of two new insured deposit products which will have significant impact on the future pricing strategies of financial institutions, as well as their profitability. These products — the money market investment account and the money market checking account — will also affect in a significant way the attractiveness of other products discussed in this book, particularly the regular savings account, the NOW account, and the regular checking account.

Financial institutions are just beginning to market these new products. So, the implications for broad restructuring of the deposit product are unclear, although many institutions have undertaken to withdraw such "bridge" products as repurchase agreements, loophole certificates, and sweep accounts. Many financial institutions have also undertaken programs to increase the service charges on other deposit accounts (e.g., regular checking and savings) in an attempt to replace some of the interest margin being eroded by the more costly money market accounts, and to weed out unprofitable accounts in an effort to help control non-interest expenses.

This chapter will examine some of the pricing fundamentals and strategies related to the new money market accounts, and will offer some guidance in the quest to create a rational and orderly product line, including money market and "regular" versions of such basic products as checking accounts and savings accounts.

The Money Market Investment Account

This product was authorized for financial institutions by the Depository Institutions Deregulation Committee (DIDC) to take effect on December 14, 1982. Its purpose was to provide insured depository institutions with a product with which to compete with money market mutual funds, which had in five years attracted over $230 billion. DIDC was instructed by Congress to create the new insured money market account after two years of strenuous debate over the changing marketplace for financial services.

Congress gave the DIDC some latitude in structuring the product, but admonished the committee that whatever it came up with had to be "competitive with and functionally equivalent to" money market funds. It was also to be insured.

After studying the potential flows of funds from money market funds and existing deposit products into a new money market deposit account, the DIDC issued the following rules relative to the new money market investment account:

- *$2,500 Minimum Balance*
  The account would have a $2,500 minimum opening and maintenance balance.
- *Interest Rate Penalty*
  If the average balance during the period of analysis (not to exceed one month) fell below $2,500, the rate of interest earned by the account would fall to the NOW account rate.

- *Limited Transactions*
  Transactions on the account would be limited to six per month, including telephone transfers, preauthorized debits or internal transfers, and third party checks. In the case of the latter, these could not exceed three of the six transactions. Personal withdrawals, however, could be made in unlimited numbers.

- *Reserves*
  For purposes of reserves computation, this account would be treated as a savings account — reservable at either 3% or 0%, depending upon whether the account holder was a corporation or an individual.

The DIDC also indicated that depository institutions were free to pay whatever rates they wished on the new account.

The Money Market Checking Account

Shortly after the DIDC authorized the new money market investment account, complaints began to grow about its transaction restrictions. Bankers felt that such limitations not only would make the account less competitive with money funds, but also felt the limitations would be extremely difficult to police.

As a result, even before the new money market investment account was introduced on December 14, 1982, DIDC authorized an unlimited transaction account version, which was initially dubbed as a "super NOW account."

This account was to be functionally identical to the money market investment account, but with two important differences:

1. *Reserves.* A uniform reserve requirement of 12% was to be imposed on all accounts.
2. *Corporations not eligible.* Due to the uncertain impact of market rate transaction accounts on bank earnings and capital, corporations would not be eligible for the new transaction account, at least not initially.

Now financial institutions had two new money market accounts to deal with: *a money market checking account* and a *money market investment account.* Additionally, during the same session at which the money market checking account was authorized, the DIDC lowered the minimum balance requirements on six month, three month, and seven- to thirty-one day certificates to $2,500, giving financial institutions a product line of money market investments with a uniform minimum balance.

Conflict of Objectives

Bankers viewed DIDC's actions with ambivalence. On the one hand, the new lineup of money market accounts could certainly be used as a weapon to attract money back from money market mutual funds. On the other hand, the ability to pay higher rates on liquid accounts would also encourage existing depositors to move money from regular savings accounts and NOW accounts, thereby significantly increasing the average cost of funds and reducing the interest margin.

In an attempt to come to grips with this difficult situation, bankers identified two key objectives to be served by short-term and longer-term pricing strategies:

1. *Win Back Money Fund Customers.* Bankers wanted to attract back the money that had gone into money funds. To do this, bankers realized that rates offered on the new accounts had to meet or exceed those offered by money funds. Market research conducted by Whittle, Raddon, Motley & Hanks, Inc. in the fall of 1982, showed that even though customers would be willing to sacrifice from 1% to 3% to obtain an insured market rate account from a local institution, inertia would tend to keep funds where they were. To overcome this, bankers elected to pay higher than market rates for a limited period as an introductory offer; then, as things settled down, gradually reduce the rate to a true market rate.

2. *Preserve Existing Low Cost Deposits.* A conflicting objective sought to preserve the funds that were currently on deposit in regular savings accounts, NOW accounts, and checking accounts. In many cases, depository institutions were earning spreads of 5% or greater on these deposits. The prospect of seeing these funds move into an account where the spread would be less than half this figure focused attention on the fact that just to maintain the same dollar amount of earnings, disregarding the negative impact on capital ratios, banks would have to attract two dollars of new money for each dollar internally converted from lower cost deposits.

Marketing Strategies Crystallized

This analysis crystallized the basic marketing strategy which most depository institutions followed. The objective called for attracting as much new money from money funds as possible, while minimizing the rate of internal conversions. Marketing strategies included several tactics:

1. *Introductory Rates.* Financial institutions introduced their money market accounts with substantial rate premiums. At a time when 91-day Treasury bills were yielding roughly 8%, depository institutions were paying customers anywhere from 9% to 21%, though these premiums were guaranteed for only a short period of time. The plan was to attract money fund customers with high initial rates, then lower the rates when much of the introductory promotional furor died down.

2. *Focused Promotion.* While many banks promoted their new accounts in the media, most engaged in a pre-introductory direct mail effort targeted to customers who were likely to have funds in a money market

mutual fund. These customers included high balance checking customers who had no savings account or certificates and others who were likely money fund users.

3. *Restrictive Fees/Penalties Below $2,500.* In an effort to preserve the existing low cost deposits, many banks also chose to minimize the promotion aimed at this portion of their deposit base while imposing stiff fees on accounts that violated the $2,500 minimum. The hope was that the combination of benign promotion and restrictive fees would discourage excessive internal conversion.

Pricing the Money Market Investment Account (Limited Access)

Pricing undoubtedly is the crucial aspect of the money market account. Determination of rates to be offered on the account, as well as fees to be charged, should reflect both short-term and long-term profit considerations. Short-term profit considerations are measured in the immediate effect of policy decision on the bottom line. Long-term considerations involve taking the necessary steps to assure that an institution is to survive. In some instances, the steps necessary to assure long-term survival conflict with those that might maximize profit in the short run.

The introduction of the money market account was fundamentally different from the NOW account introduction. The key to this difference is that NOW pricing decisions affected only a portion of the market, basically those in the $200 to $1,500 balance range. High balance customers, those responsible for the bulk of deposit dollars, were not affected by pricing decisions, since all financial institutions were limited to paying 5¼%. Hence, these customers made their NOW account decision based upon factors other than rate, i.e., convenience, reputation, or service. Commercial banks could trade on the fact that they owned the market and concentrate on maintaining profitability, knowing that their pricing policies would not result in a major outflow of funds, and at the same time export some portion of their unprofitable transaction accounts to the thrifts. Thrifts, on the other hand, viewed the lower balance accounts as essentially new money to invest in the higher rate investment alternatives.

The entrance of totally deregulated rates into the competitive framework created a different environment. With rate as a competitive factor, all accounts are subject to pricing decisions and are vulnerable to competitors paying a higher rate, especially at introduction.

A Few Considerations

The profitability of any account depends upon four factors:

1. The cost incurred by the bank in the maintenance of that account
2. The level of balances maintained in the account
3. The rate spread between the sources and uses of those balances
4. Explicit fees levied on the account

Even in a completely deregulated environment, some degree of differentiation between institutions will always be attainable. Convenience, reputation, and service factors will play some role, albeit perhaps reduced, in the financial industry. As a consequence, some disparity in rate between various institutions offering the same, or nearly the same, product may be tolerated. However, for the most part, any differential will not be large. By the same line of reasoning, large differences in explicit fees will not be tolerated. Thus, the importance of streamlining operations in order to reduce operational costs and increase profit margins can be seen. A critical need in a deregulated environment will be control over non-interest expenditures.

Similarly, in a deregulated environment subsidization of low balance, unprofitable customers by high balance customers cannot be tolerated. If high balance customers are required to subsidize low balance accounts, rates paid to high balance accounts will have to be reduced, which may result in the loss of those accounts. Every customer should be required to pay for the services they receive. Traditionally, more affluent customers pay for their service implicitly, through a slight reduction in the rate on the balances they maintain. Low balance customers, on the other hand, generally do not maintain sufficient balance levels, so that operating costs can be implicitly covered by balance-derived revenue. Therefore, they should be charged an explicit fee to offset operating costs.

Finally, institutions need to develop some stringent guidelines in regard to asset-liability management, especially if the rate fluctuation of the past few years' magnitude continues. The decision to maintain a positive or negative gap or to match assets and liabilities closely in terms of maturity will be extremely crucial. If a gap is maintained and the asset-liability committee has guessed correctly on the direction of rates, the result may be greatly enhanced profitability. On the other hand, an incorrect guess as to the direction of rates will have the opposite effect. The rate received on the bank's investments would fall below market rates and, therefore, the rate payable to depositors would fall below that of other institutions. The bank at that point could either pay competitive rates to its depositors or not pay competitive rates and run the risk of disintermediation. In either case, the effect would be a decline in earnings.

Costs

The first step in pricing any product is an examination of cost/revenue relationships. As has been discussed throughout this book, it is important to separate costs into functional (or operating) costs and interest (or money) costs.

The average monthly operating costs of a Money Market Investment Account are based upon assumptions which, of course, should be modified to reflect your situation:

- Monthly statements (similar to checking accounts)
- Two deposits per month
- Three checks per month

For a typical middle-sized bank the costs of those functions and the related volumes would produce this monthly cost profile:

Activity	Cost Per Item	Monthly Activity	Monthly Cost
Account maintenance	$3.24	1	$3.24
Checks	$ .12	3	$ .36
Deposits	$ .25	2	$ .50
Total cost			$4.10

Translated into a yearly figure, this operating cost would total roughly $50 per year ($4.10 × 12 = $49.20) (based upon Functional Cost Data).

The next step in the process involves translating this cost into an equivalent interest margin requirement, since this cost must be recovered to some extent by the difference between what a bank earns on the funds invested versus what it pays its depositors. This interest margin might be referred to as the "spread to breakeven," since it is what is required to cover the operating costs. For example, if a customer opened a $2,500 money market account, you could pay him or her 2% less than you earn by investing his deposit ($50 ÷ $2,500 = 2%).

As we can see from the following chart, the larger the customer's deposit, the lower the spread to breakeven, since the operating costs are fixed.

Investable Balance	Operating Cost	Spread to Breakeven
$50,000	$50	.1 %
$20,000	$50	.25%
$10,000	$50	.50%
$ 5,000	$50	1.00%
$ 2,000	$50	2.50%

Clearly, the larger a customer's balance, the more yield we can "pass through" from your assets to your liabilities.

Of course, no bank wants to just breakeven. So we must also expand our required spread by a profit factor. If, for example, our profit target is 1% return on assets and our capital to asset ratio is 10%, then we must earn 1.11% on our deposit liabilities. Of course, not all liabilities are burdened with the same rate sensitivity, so we may elect to pursue a profit spread of 2% on some sources of funds (e.g., checking) and ½% on others (e.g., money market accounts).

In our example and for illustrative purposes, we'll pursue a .75% profit spread over operating costs as an initial objective and plan to increase that spread in the future when we suspect that rate sensitivity may be lower.

Offering Rate Influenced By Balance Level

Using this concept of required spread, the accounts arranged by size as in Table 3.11 could offer rates based upon the interest margins.

TABLE 3.11   Rate Table Based on Interest Margin.

Average Balance	Spread to Breakeven	+	Profit Margin	=	Total Spread
$50,000	.1 %		.75%		.85%
$20,000	.25%		.75%		1.00%
$10,000	.50%		.75%		·1.25%
$ 5,000	1.00%		.75%		1.75%
$ 2,000	2.50%		.75%		3.25%

Such a chart suggests that a bank can afford to be more competitive (i.e., pay a higher rate) to customers who have larger balances. As a result, it is very common to see a pricing structure for money market accounts featuring a tiered set of rates.

Average Balance	Rate	Fees
Over $20,000	10.25%	None
$10,000 to $20,000	9.85%	None
$ 2,500 to $10,000	9.00%	None
Below $2,500	5¼%	$6.00 plus $.20 per check

Such a structure gives preference to larger denomination accounts, allows a highly promotable rate, and discourages smaller accounts.

Offering Rate Influenced By Matched Asset

So far, our pricing considerations have focused on the required spread. Except for the previous illustration, we have not discussed the actual rate a customer would receive. This is because in a deregulated environment, the rate paid to the customer is dependent upon the investment philosophy and orientation of the bank. Indeed, it has been observed that the "silver bullet" of deregulation is yield on assets, and that the bank which can best maximize its yield on assets on an ongoing basis will be in a competitively advantageous position.

Asset & Liability Management

While it is beyond the scope of this book to explore the intricacies of asset and liability management, it is important to note the disparity in yields of various short-term investments. On any given day it is not at all unusual to see a 300 basis point difference between Fed Funds and the commercial prime rate, with other short-term investments such as Treasury securities and Bankers Acceptances somewhere in between.

Of course, much of the money attracted into money market accounts will behave like a core deposit and remain in the bank throughout the interest rate cycle. This opens up the possibility of mismatching maturities to take advantage of even higher longer-term investment yields.

The point is, in a deregulated environment each bank will have its own investment philosophy and its own resulting yield on matched or mismatched assets.

After you've made your basic philosophical decision about where you're going to invest the money, use the principles in this chapter to help determine what you can afford to pay for the underlying deposits. And if you are unhappy with this rate, you may have to focus additional attention on the adequacy of the basic investment assumptions. In other words, if you'd prefer to invest in Fed Funds and pay your depositors 7% when everyone else is paying 8%, you may have to go out and develop more commercial loans.

Competition

Studies done by the Federal Reserve in early 1983 show that a substantial amount of money is flowing back into banks from money market funds as a result of this new product. In early December 1982, money market funds reached their all time high of approximately $240 billion. By April of 1983, this figure was down to $178 billion, with the majority of the decline going into bank money market accounts.

During this period, banks and thrifts generally paid higher rates than the money funds; but the differential began to narrow after the first month.

Research done by Whittle, Raddon, Motley & Hanks, Inc., shows that a majority of money market investors would keep their funds in their local bank rather than a money fund, even if the funds paid a slightly higher rate.

This relationship is still in a state of flux, but bankers should watch the relationships between their own deposit rates and those of other banks and money funds.

The Donoghue Organization of Holliston, MA, publishes information on the rates paid by money funds. And the Bank Administration Institute, Rolling Meadows, Illinois, monitors the rates paid by banks on deregulated accounts through an electronic service called "Money Market Monitor."

The Money Market Checking Account

The pricing of the money market checking account is similar to pricing the investment account, except for some additional factors.

Higher Operating Costs. Instead of $50.00 a year, the operating costs of a personal money market checking account will be in the neighborhood of $80 (see Chapter 1, "Checking Account Costs"). This will result in a "spread to breakeven" of:

Average Balance	Functional Cost	Spread to Breakeven
$50,000	$80	.16%
$20,000	$80	.40%
$10,000	$80	.80%
$ 5,000	$80	1.60%
$ 2,000	$80	4.00%

Reserves. A uniform 12% reserve requirement means that only $.88 of each depositor's dollar is actually invested. If the bank's profit objective is to earn 75% on this source of funds, it must actually increase the profit margin to .85% (.75 ÷ .88). Consequently, the total spread on a money market checking account would look like this:

Average Balance	Breakeven Spread	+	Profit Margin	=	Total Spread
$50,000	.16%		.85%		1.01%
$20,000	.40%		.85%		1.25%
$10,000	.80%		.85%		1.65%
$ 5,000	1.60%		.85%		2.45%
$ 2,000	4.00%		.85%		4.85%

Comparing the spread on the money market investment account, we see the total required spread to earn .75%.

Average Balance	Money Market Investment Account	Money Market Checking Account	Difference
$50,000	.85%	1.01%	.16%
$20,000	1.00%	1.25%	.25%
$10,000	1.25%	1.65%	.40%
$ 5,000	1.75%	2.45%	.70%
$ 2,000	3.25%	4.85%	1.60%

Clearly, money market checking accounts should pay less than money market investment accounts. You may elect to use a similar tiered structure and peg the rate to your money market investment account; or alternatively, use the money market investment rate itself less, say ½%, across the board.

The idea that a money market checking account should pay less than a money market investment account is also quite consistent with consumer attitudes about the perceived value of immediate and unlimited liquidity.

Pricing Structure. There are basically two alternate ways to charge for the checkwriting feature of a money market checking account. The traditional approach (as outlined above) suggests that the costs of the checkwriting be absorbed by the interest margin, so the customer does not have to pay a service charge. Of course, implicit in the approach is a lower yield to the customer for his invested funds.

An example of such a structure would be:

Minimum Balance	Rate	Fee
Over $20,000	9.25%	None
$10,000 to $20,000	8.85%	None
$ 2,500 to $10,000	8.00%	None
Below $2,500	5.25%	$10 plus $.20 per check

This structure allows a more attractive rate at the high balance range than would be possible if all accounts over $2,500 earned the same rate. And while there would be some sacrifice of simplicity, the market for which this product is structured is sophisticated enough to prefer the rate reward for higher balances.

It is important to understand that even though you may be paying a higher rate to higher balance customers, such rate is still reflective of an interest margin wide enough to absorb $80 per year of operating costs.

An alternative is to pay a higher rate to the customer (i.e., operate on a lower spread) and charge a checkwriting fee. Such a plan would permit higher offering rates but would also necessitate a fee, which many customers find bothersome. If this latter approach is used, either by itself or with the minimum balance concept, it is recommended that a "loaded" activity cost be used (see Chapter 1).

Other Pricing Considerations

Frequency of Rate Change
The frequency of rate change is correlated with the frequency of change in the yield of the matching asset. If deposits gathered through this account are invested in new issues of Treasury Bills, then the rate offered on the account might fluctuate weekly. If, on the other hand, deposits are invested in loans that are re-priced monthly, then theoretically the rate should change monthly.

With additional experience, it is likely that deposits from money market accounts will be invested in a variety of short-term investments. In this event, it is probably wise to reserve the right to change the rate daily, even though in practice you may not. This additional flexibility will allow you to adjust rates more rapidly when rates are falling than when they are rising, thus improving your overall profitability.

Ledger vs. Collected vs. Investable Balances
Always use investable balances if possible, otherwise you will have to lower your offering rate accordingly.

Commercial Accounts
Commercial accounts using any type of money market account or related cash management service should be put on a strict account analysis. Activity costs may then be recovered by the customer's choice of non-earning balances of an adequate level or direct fees.

Product Line Structure
With the addition of the money market accounts, much of the interest rate deregulation long forecast is in place. There will undoubtedly be additional functional deregulation (i.e., the modification of Glass-Steagall), but for purposes of structuring deposit products the basic structure is now pretty clear. The deposit products really sort themselves into three broad groups: transaction accounts, savings accounts, and investment accounts. Following is a description of a basic product line in each group and a discussion of its intended purpose or market.

Transaction Accounts

1. *Regular Checking.* This account is for the mass market customer who keeps relatively little in his account and who is looking primarily for convenient, efficient access to his spending funds.
2. *Money Market Checking.* This account is for the affluent customer who keeps a substantial sum in his account for "comfort zone" reasons and who wants to earn something on his idle funds. The rate paid on this account, however, should be lower than that offered on the money market investment account with limited access.

    There can be business versions of both of these products.
3. *NOW Account.* Many banks elected not to convert NOW accounts to the money market checking account, because to do so might have resulted in paying

well in excess of 5¼% to many customers who would not have converted. Such a strategy is smart in the short run, but in the longer run NOW accounts should probably be eliminated to promote a more rational and simplified product line. Consideration should be given to mass conversion of these accounts to regular checking status, with a customer initiated alternative of conversion to money market status.

Investment Accounts

1. *Money Market Investment Account.* This is the market rate account for people who want maximum liquidity. Typically, it pays a rate higher than the money market checking account, but less than term certificates. Also, higher balances earn more attractive rates.
2. *Term Certificates.* These certificates should be issued in maturities that match typical liquidity preferences. For example:

   - one month
   - three months
   - six months
   - one year
   - two years

   The rates offered should, of course, reflect investment opportunities, but in periods when the yield curve is normal they should rise as the maturity lengthens.
3. *Asset Management Account.* To further solidify the bank's relationship with its high balance customer base, many banks are offering so-called asset management accounts, which bring all of a customer's accounts (and often even outside investments) together into a portfolio depicted on one monthly or quarterly statement. Such accounts are sold as part of a total

relationship, often including an assigned banker, or "deposit counselor," whose job it is to help customers match investment alternatives to risk and liquidity preference.

Savings Accounts

While savings account dollars will continue to convert to investment accounts, there remains a legitimate need for the regular savings account for two basic reasons. First, the idea of a fixed rate, liquid account is appealing to a sizeable segment of the "non-rate sensitive" market. Second, many customers simply do not have enough money in their accounts to earn market rates without sizeable offsetting fees.

4

Monitoring Prices

Pricing competitively and profitably is one of the most important functions in a bank. To ensure that this is done properly, your bank should have a formal and systematic pricing review procedure; and to work most effectively this procedure should have four basic components.

1. A pricing committee with responsibility for reviewing prices and recommending changes
2. A system for gathering, analyzing, and reporting key *cost, volume,* and *revenue data*
3. A general pricing policy
4. A set of forms, rules, and procedures to bring together all the pertinent variables.

The purpose of this chapter is to describe an approach for establishing an overall pricing system.

Step 1:   Form a pricing committee

Step 2:   Develop a way to gather cost, volume, and revenue data

Step 3:   Formulate a pricing policy

Step 4:   Develop a set of forms, rules, and procedures

THE PRICING COMMITTEE

A bank is an organization of many functions which often combines talents to produce a product. The Functional Cost Analysis Program of the Fed helps put this into perspective, and offers a rationale for determining how these functional costs combine into a product cost.

Since many people from different organizational units within the bank are involved in producing financial products, it makes sense that a bank should form a committee to help review existing prices and to establish new ones.

This chapter will lay out the basic philosophy, organization, and operational functions of a pricing committee. And while the composition of our example committee may reflect a larger bank, the basic approach has worked in banks with as little as $25 million in deposits.

Overview

The Pricing Committee is a broadly constituted group of bank employees charged by top management with determining, implementing, and monitoring a pricing policy designed to maximize bank profits within the context of, and constraints imposed by, the bank's overall earnings and growth goals.

Following is a description of the composition of the committee and the functions of the various elements.

Step 1. The Pricing Committee

The pricing committee is a broadly constituted standing committee charged by top mangement with the responsibility to determine, implement, and monitor the bank's pricing policy and practices.

For the pricing committee to operate effectively it is important that its membership reflect those functional areas of the bank that affect overall bank earnings. This effect on bank earnings (and the related composition of the committee) must take account of both revenues and costs. Consequently, the pricing committee must be composed of individuals whose primary responsibility is to ensure efficient, low cost functioning of products.

To ensure that various recommendations of the pricing committee (with top management approval) are supported throughout the bank, and to ensure that input to the decision process is representative, the pricing committee should be constituted to include individuals from the following areas:

- Accounting
- Branch Administration
- Data Processing
- Lending
- Marketing
- Operations
- Trust

The specific composition of the pricing committee shall be determined by and subject to review by top management.

The Chairman

Administrative functioning of the pricing committee shall be the responsibility of the chairman, who is appointed by top management.

It is the chairman's responsibility to:

1. Ensure that the bank has a well understood pricing policy
2. Ensure that all products are priced in accordance with the bank's pricing policy
3. Ensure that implementation of price changes occurs in a timely fashion
4. Ensure that top management understands and approves all actions of the committee
5. Ensure that all products receive periodic price reviews

To achieve these objectives, the chairman shall administer and be responsible for the mechanics of the pricing committee. These mechanics include:

1. Bi-weekly meetings of the committee to review a prioritized agenda of services whose prices are candidates for change
2. Voting procedures
3. Functioning of the Cost/Volume/Revenue (CVR) task force which is responsible for gathering information from which the committee will make its judgments
4. The maintenance of a prioritized list of products whose prices are to be reviewed

Step 2. The Cost/Volume/Revenue Task Force

The CVR task force is narrowly constituted of analysis technicians responsible to the chairman of the pricing committee for developing the necessary information required by the pricing committee in conformance with:

a. The bank's pricing policy
b. Administrative procedures outlined in "The Pricing Mechanism."

The CVR task force shall be made up of a *minimum* number of people who are skilled and experienced in the development and utilization of cost/volume/profit information. The specific number of analysts working within the task force (either temporarily, part-time, or full time) shall be determined by the chairman of the pricing committee and be based upon projected product analysis work.

To ensure that the CVR task force operates efficiently, the chairman of the pricing committee shall appoint a task force leader. It shall be his or her responsibility to:

- Assemble all information called for on the Pricing Input Form for each product identified by the committee for review during each quarter. One month prior to the end of each quarter, the pricing committee shall establish which products are to be reviewed during the ensuing quarter and prioritize them on the Product Analysis & Review Schedule. Then, the chairman of the pricing committee and the leader of the CVR task force shall establish those committee meeting dates for the review of specific products, based upon an estimate of the time required to generate the necessary cost/volume/revenue data.

- Complete the data gathering effort in a timely fashion consistent with "time vs. manpower" trade-offs established by the chairman of the pricing committee.

- Attend all pricing committee meetings.

- Record and publish minutes of all pricing committee meetings.

Step 3. Pricing Policy

The initial function of the pricing committee is to develop the bank's written pricing policy. Once this is developed, the committee should review it periodically (at least yearly) to ensure that it remains consistent with the bank's profit/growth objectives.

The bank's pricing policy is a written document detailing the policy of the bank regarding the pricing of its various products and services.

The policy is to be developed, monitored, and implemented by the pricing committee with specific approval of top management. It should articulate the bank's philosophy regarding a number of factors related to pricing and be in harmony with the bank's profit and growth goals.

Top management must take an active role in the development of the pricing policy.

Pricing policy should be broad enough to allow the pricing committee some latitude to meet day-to-day profitability and competitive situations, yet narrow enough to express top management's overriding strategic plan.

Following are some topical areas which should be addressed in a bank's pricing policy.

1. *Fees vs. Balances*
   If the bank has a preference, it should be articulated. If customers are allowed a choice, the bank's preference should be built into the conversion formula.
2. *Collected vs. Investible vs. Ledger*
3. *Costs/Volume/Revenue/Profit Dynamics*
   What costs are assigned to a product. What volume and revenues are necessary to achieve profit targets. What minimum is acceptable return on investment criteria; what is the necessary pay back period for new products.
4. *Credit*

   - Define the role of compensating balances.
   - Is credit availability a product?
   - How are customer lending rates set?

5. *Product Pricing vs. Customer Relationship Pricing*

6. *New Products*

- Performance criteria
- Timing

7. *Role of Pricing vis-a-vis Other Marketing Elements*

- Promotion
- Distribution
- Product Differentiation

Pricing Techniques

Based upon an articulation of the bank's posture with regard to each issue in Step 3, the bank should define its preferred pricing technique for products sold to each major market:

- Commercial
- Personal
- Correspondent
- Public Funds
- Trust
- Investments

Each of the various loan, deposit, investment, or activity services delivered to these markets should be considered when determining the bank's preferred pricing technique, selected from these alternatives:

1. markup over variable cost
2. markup over total average cost at projected volume
3. competitive pricing (at the market)
4. above the market (skimming)
5. below the market (penetration)

Given the bank's different competitive postures in each market, different pricing strategies may be called for.

Step 4. The Pricing Mechanism

The pricing mechanism describes how the various components of the system interact. The mechanism is made up of a series of rules governing the conduct of the committee, the CVR task force, and top management.

Supporting this mechanism is a series of data forms to be completed by the CVR task force to aid committee members in making their decisions.

Following is a sample write-up of committee rules and voting procedures, as well as a set of data forms. Please recognize that these are examples only and are not intended to limit the structure of your pricing mechanism.

A SAMPLE WRITE-UP OF COMMITTEE RULES AND VOTING PROCEDURES

Sample Data Forms

Product Analysis and Review Schedule

This form is maintained by the chairman of the pricing committee. Its purpose is to inform all interested parties which products are scheduled for review during any quarter. The chairman may elect to maintain a running four-quarter agenda to insure an orderly flow and to allow for adequate analysis time by the CVR task force.

Pricing Input Form

This data form is to be completed by the CVR task force and provided to committee members prior to each meeting. Its purpose is to assemble all of the information relevant to the pricing decision on a *specific product*.

Pricing Recommendation Summary

This form is the output of the committee. It is the committee's specific pricing recommendation relative to a specific product. It goes to top management for final ratification.

Product Analysis and Review Schedule
Products to be reviewed by Pricing Committee during
_____ quarter of 1983.

Product	Date of Last Review	Anticipated Analysis Time	Priority* A,B,C	Estimated Date of Review

*Priority A = Significant impact on overall bank profitability.
Priority B = Moderate impact on overall bank profitability.
Priority C = Minor impact on overall bank profitability.

Pricing Recommendation Summary

☐ New Product
☐ Product Review
☐ Special Attention

Product: _____

Date: _____

Recommendation:

_____

_____

_____

Date of Implementation _____

Reason for Change:

_____

_____

_____

_____

Cost/Volume/Profit:

	'82	'83	'84	'85	'86
Recommended Price	___	___	___	___	___
Estimated Volume (Annual)	___	___	___	___	___
Gross Revenue	___	___	___	___	___
Total Cost	___	___	___	___	___
Net Margin	___	___	___	___	___

Elasticity of Demand Summary

_____

_____

_____

Anticipated Competitive Action

_____

_____

_____

_____

Implementation Procedures

_____

_____

_____

_____

_____

Pricing Worksheet

This worksheet is to be completed for each product to be considered by the Pricing Committee. It contains the detail supporting the "Pricing Recommendation Summary."

I. *The Product*
    A. Product Name and Description of Customer Benefits

    _____

    _____

    _____

    B. Substitute Products — Products which could be used in place of product under evaluation.

    _____

    _____

    _____

II. *Market Conditions*

    A. Current Competitive Prices

                Institution   *Price*

         _____   _____

         _____   _____

         _____   _____

         _____   _____

         _____   _____

         _____   _____

         _____   _____

    B. Competitor reactions to changes in the past — interpretation of pricing strategy.

                Institution   *Pricing Reaction/Strategy*

         _____   _____

         _____   _____

         _____   _____

         _____   _____

         _____   _____

         _____   _____

         _____   _____

III. *Cost/Volume/Revenue Data*

    A. Fixed cost allocated to product per year _____

    _____

    B. Share of other division expenses (overhead) per year allocated to product _____

    _____

    C. Variable cost(s) _____

    _____

    _____

    D. Volume: Current per year _____

    E. Current share of market for each competitor _____

    _____

    F. Growth rate in total market _____

    _____

    G. Breakeven point(s): $\dfrac{\text{Fixed Cost}}{\text{Price} - \text{Variable Cost}}$

    At current price (or proposal price for new service)

    _____

    H. Mark-up percent over current variable cost _____

    _____

IV. *Elasticity of Demand Summary*

	Price	Volume	Revenue	Cost	Profit
+50%	_____	_____	_____	_____	_____
+40%	_____	_____	_____	_____	_____
+30%	_____	_____	_____	_____	_____
+20%	_____	_____	_____	_____	_____
+10%	_____	_____	_____	_____	_____
Current	_____	_____	_____	_____	_____
−10%	_____	_____	_____	_____	_____
−20%	_____	_____	_____	_____	_____
−30%	_____	_____	_____	_____	_____
−40%	_____	_____	_____	_____	_____
−50%	_____	_____	_____	_____	_____

V. *Impact of Other Factors for Consideration*

A. Technological

B. Legislative/Regulatory

C. Competitive

D. Economic

E. Internal

VI. *Product History*

Date of introduction _____

Date of last price change _____

Nature of last change _____

_____

Volume in 1982 _____	Market Share in 1982 _____
1981 _____	1981 _____
1980 _____	1980 _____
1979 _____	1979 _____
1978 _____	1978 _____
1977 _____	1977 _____

Current position in product life cycle and predicted evolution

_____

_____

_____

_____

_____

VII. *Recommendations*

	'78	'79	'80	'81	'82
Recommended Price					
Estimated Volume (Annual)					
Gross Revenue (Annual)					
Total Cost of Projected Volume					
Net Margin					

VIII. *Implementation*

What is your recommended implementation procedure?

_____

_____

_____

_____

Date of implementation _____

Index